THE GOOD LEADERSHIP BOOK

AAMER NAEEM AND MARIA PATTINSON

Copyright © 2025 by Aamer Naeem and Maria Pattinson.

All rights reserved.

The right of Aamer Naeem and Maria Pattinson to be identified as the authors of this work has been asserted in accordance with the Copyright, Design and Patents Act 1998.

A catalogue record for this book is available from the British Library
ISBN: 978-1-0684664-0-3 (paperback)
ISBN: 978-1-0684664-1-0 (ebook)

All rights reserved. The book is copyright. Subject to statutory exceptions and the provisions of relevant collective licensing agreements, no reproduction of any part may take place without the written permission of the authors.

First Edition: May 2025

www.goodleadership.org

AUTHORS

Aamer Naeem OBE: Aamer has over two decades of senior leadership experience. He has held Directorships and Chief Executive positions in multinational and multimillion-pound organisations. A qualified pharmacist, he completed his Master's in Business Administration, with Distinction, from Nottingham University Business School. He has sat as a Fitness to Practice Committee Member on the General Pharmaceutical Council of Great Britain and the General  Teaching Council for England. Having trained and coached hundreds of leaders, he has vast experience across private, public, and voluntary sectors. His work in building leaders and organisations has allowed him to deliver his leadership development programmes and coaching globally across 5 continents. In 2019 he was awarded an OBE in the Queen's New Year Honours List and featured in the Green Park BAME 100 Business Leaders Index.

Maria Pattinson: Maria is an Ethical Leadership and Communication specialist. She has thirty years of experience coaching individuals and teams to become the best versions of themselves. Maria brings expertise in mental health and wellbeing, having delivered projects to improve mental health outcomes for communities in the UK and internationally. She has a first-class Master's in Ethical Leadership from King's College London.  Maria coaches teams in the international development context, especially in East Africa and Iraq. For over twenty years, Maria worked with top leaders in the NHS flagship programmes run by The King's Fund, developing leadership capacity to communicate authentically and effectively in public. Her coaching and facilitation draw upon an equally long career as a theatre director and producer of new plays in some of England's leading theatre organisations, including Chichester Festival Theatre, Glyndebourne and Hampstead Theatre. Maria has written about the intersection of leadership, the arts and transformation, and is trained in Systemic Constellations Coaching and Family Constellations.

> "What you seek is seeking you."
>
> **Rumi**

CONTENTS

AUTHORS	3
CHAPTER 1. SETTING UP	7
Stepping Up	9
Levelling Up and Joining Up	10
Showing Up	11
The Three Domains of Leadership	12
The Four Dimensions of Leadership	13
CHAPTER 2. STEPPING UP AND GROWING UP	15
Characters in the Domain of Self	19
Characters in the Domain of Others	44
Characters in the Domain of Context	72
CHAPTER 3. LEVELLING UP AND JOINING UP	101
Levelling Up to become Specialists	103
Joining Up Specialists to release Virtue Practitioners	108
Master Practitioners	148
CHAPTER 4. SHOWING UP	151
Jacinda Ardern	154
Yusuf Cat Stevens	157
Poppy Jaman	160
CHAPTER 5. SUMMING UP	163

Continue the Good Leadership Journey online at:
https://www.goodleadership.org
https://www.facebook.com/TheGoodLeadershipBook
https://www.instagram.com/goodleadershipbook
https://x.com/goodleadershipb
https://www.youtube.com/goodleadership
https://www.linkedin.com/in/goodleadershipbook

DEDICATION

*Dedicated to two strong women who have been leaders
and role models in our lives.*

Naz Coker

&

Balqis Akhter Naeem

Their light continues to shine

CHAPTER 1
SETTING UP

"*A stage setting is not a background; it is an environment.*"
Robert Edmond Jones

SETTING UP

The world is crying out for Good Leadership. This book is about learning what a Good Leader is, and how to become one. We make the process of becoming a Good Leader more digestible and achievable. We unlock your leadership potential to respond to individual and collective challenges with awareness, integrity, creativity and clarity.

The great acting teacher Konstantin Stanislavski is noted for describing to students that the way to approach a new role is the same as you would approach eating a turkey. You must carve it into slices and not attempt to digest it whole. This segmentation makes the whole much easier to absorb. This is the learning journey that you are about to start. We will take Good Leadership and carve it into the Twelve Essential Characters for ease. We will then build up the model through exploring the relationship between the Characters.

The Journey begins by **Stepping Up** into the Twelve Core Characters and then **Growing Up** to develop them further. **Levelling Up** and **Joining Up** allow you to enhance them, and to conclude, we showcase Good Leadership, through example, in the chapter entitled **Showing Up**.

Stepping Up

"You cannot dream yourself into a character;
you must hammer and forge yourself one."
Henry David Thoreau

We introduce you to the Twelve Characters essential to Good Leadership, allowing them to 'step up' onto their stage. These Twelve Characters are leadership archetypes that have a universal recognition. They operate in one of three environments: The Domain of Self Leadership, also referred to as the inner Domain; the Domain of Others, which concerns relationships; and the Domain of Context, relating to more complex organisations, communities, and societies. They also reside in their respective 'homes' or Dimensions of Leadership. These are the Dimensions of Understanding, Ethics, Purpose and Communication. These Twelve Characters form a map, allowing you to evaluate your personal leadership, and that of others, against a desirable standard.

> *"Knowing is not enough; we must apply.*
> *Willing is not enough; we must do."*
> **Johann Wolfgang von Goethe**

We then guide you on how to develop your Characters further, allowing them to 'grow up,' so you can 'do' them better. We show you how to bring the mind, heart, body and spirit to each. How to develop the 4Ls of Depth: Learn, Love, Lead and Live the Characters; how to build familiarity, passion, integrity and competence in each. As an actor would learn to embody a role in a play and so become credible and impactful; similarly, a leader can call upon the developed Twelve Characters to become more credible and impactful too.

Levelling Up and Joining Up

> *"Alone we can do so little; together we can do so much."*
> **Helen Keller**

We explore what happens as the Characters come together with those in the same Dimension. As you develop all three Characters in a Dimension, you 'level up' to become a Specialist in that Dimension. That is, an Understanding Specialist, an Ethical Specialist, a Purpose Specialist, and a Communication Specialist.

The interplay between the Characters of different Dimensions is then explored. This 'joining up' shows how 'together they can do so much more.' Working in tandem, the collaboration of the Characters unleashes Leadership Virtues. The Practitioners of these Leadership Virtues are shown to be either Wise, Courageous, Prudent, Social, Spiritual or Just. We also look at the potential shadows of leadership,

Leadership Vices and Blind Spots, that reveal due to the underdevelopment of certain Characters. Here you will find guidance on what needs to be done to prevent them from getting in the way of you achieving positive outcomes for yourself and those you influence.

Showing Up

"Example is leadership."
Albert Schweitzer

We end your journey by showcasing Good Leadership. We present how Good Leaders 'show up' all around. Three contemporary leaders are chosen as examples of the combined Leadership Virtues in practice.

"The illiterate of the 21st century will not be those who cannot read and write, but those who cannot learn, unlearn and relearn."
Alvin Toffier

The Good Leadership Model we are presenting draws upon three decades of experience as organisational leaders, coaches, and facilitators of leadership development programmes around the globe. Our work together has been fuelled by a drive to find a framework that is comprehensive enough to articulate 'the way' of a Good Leader. Leadership development programmes are a good catalyst for a journey of personal exploration and growth, but are often only the start.

Our journey looks at what needs to happen once this catalytic moment has passed. What is the pathway that the Good Leader treads? How can a person assess whether they are on the way? And perhaps most importantly, as learning and development professionals, what additional guidance will help leaders stay connected to their leadership journey? This Good Leadership Model is the result of that enquiry.

In our unpredictable world, people and organisations have a great deal of change coming at them very fast. Leaders need to be equipped to respond and respond with speed. There seems to be little time to learn on the job. They need to be able to adapt to the environment and challenges presented to them. Stock responses, based on personality, habits and preferences, fall short. Leaders are in danger of repeating the mistakes of the past or lacking relevance to the present and future. Inflexibility and persona led profiles, for example, Margaret Thatcher's 'Iron Lady' or Donald Trump's 'Strong Man,' just will not do. What happens if the situation requires patience and compassion? Does this mean that the tough talker has become weak? Not at all! Guiding through change is the business of leadership, and flexibility around learning and unlearning is implied. Good Leaders need to be more than one-dimensional. The Good Leadership Model equips you to be responsive in your leadership journey - our complex world demands it.

The Three Domains of Leadership

These are the three environments of leadership: Self, Others and Context.

The Domain of Self is the area of leadership that pertains to our inner attitudes, thoughts, beliefs, and feelings. The ability to reflect upon who we are, what we stand for and where we are going. It links to the way we lead ourselves, manage our internal discussions and own our inner shadows.

The Domain of Others is the area of leadership that pertains to the way we present ourselves to others. It reflects the way we manage relationships and build capacity in the people around us. It is the arena of our behaviours with family members, subordinates, and teams.

The Domain of Context is the area of leadership that pertains to the systems that we are in. It may be organisations, communities, or society at large; Institutions and stakeholders that you seek to influence or are influenced by. Leadership is most commonly perceived as operating in this Domain. It is the ability to zoom out and take the wide-angled view of a situation; ask questions about what is hidden from view and then zoom in to see from the ground upwards and then use this knowledge to have a wider desired impact on your system.

Strong roots in the inner Domains allow more stretch in the outer Domains. They provide both the foundation and the agility to make the right choices for wider leadership challenges. When you develop the four Characters in a Domain, you become a leader of that Domain.

That is a leader of the Domain of Self, the Domain of Others, or the Domain of Context.

The Four Dimensions of Leadership

These are the four areas of leadership competence: Understanding, Ethics, Purpose, and Communication.

Understanding is a mental and emotional process. It enables you to make rational assessments based upon the accuracy of your comprehension and perception. It relies on experience and precedence. It looks at the relationship between people, objects and other systems. At the heart of the Understanding Dimension is the question: Who or what needs to be known in this situation? It provides the clarity needed to enable informed choices and actions.

Ethics is the part of leadership that covers morality. The principles that govern your thoughts, attitudes, and actions. It is concerned with values and what is right. It demands the consideration of intentions, means and consequences. It assesses endeavours in terms of integrity, sustainability, and wholesome growth. At the heart of the Ethical Dimension is the question: What is right and wrong? What do we need to think, feel, and do to hold this true for us and others?

Purpose provides direction to the leadership effort. It is the resolve or determination to do or achieve something that is meaningful. It is what gets you out of bed in the morning and working late into the night. It provides energy, motivation, creativity and inspiration. In organisational terms, Purpose is often expressed as a 'vision statement,' a proclamation of a Purpose achieved. At the heart of the Purpose Dimension are the questions: Where are we going? What do we need to do to get there? Who else can help?

Communication is about imparting or exchanging information. It can involve different modes like reflecting, speaking, and writing. It can involve multiple platforms such as meetings, broadcasting, social and global media. It is through Communication that feelings, thoughts, actions, and intentions are conveyed. The way something is communicated is as important as its content. The selection of tone, body language, pitch and platform will all impact on the message received. At the heart of the Communication Dimension is the question: What needs to be seen and heard?

When you develop the three Characters in a Dimension, you become a Specialist in that Dimension. That is, an Understanding Specialist, an Ethical Specialist, a Purpose Specialist, and a Communication Specialist. These four Dimensions of Good Leadership combine with the three Domains to complete a wheel that gives us a framework of learning.

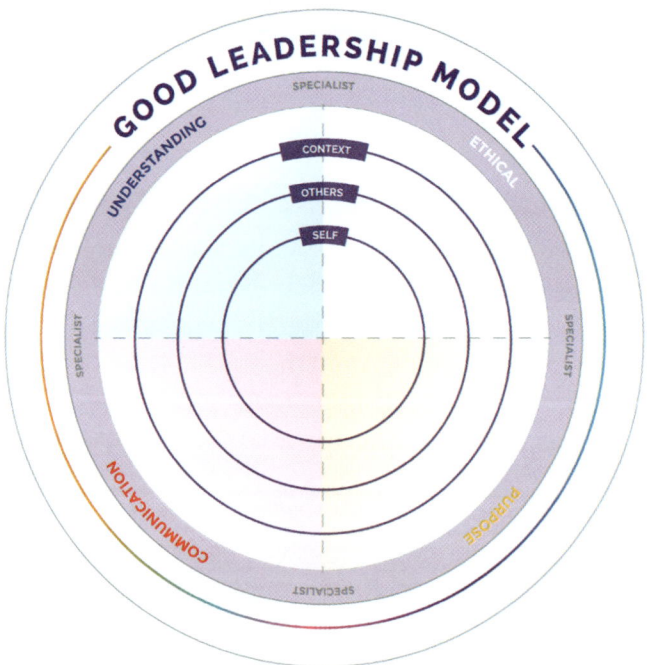

CHAPTER 2
STEPPING UP AND GROWING UP

"*Once you stop learning, you start dying*"
Albert Einstein

STEPPING UP AND GROWING UP

Let's take a closer look at the Twelve Characters as they 'step up' onto the stage of Good Leadership. Who are they? What do they say and do? What do they look like? What are their stories and roles in Good Leadership?

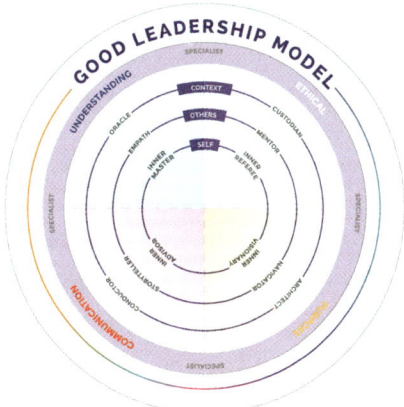

We share how to help them 'grow up' into Characters with Depth, allowing their practice to become more natural. With Depth, they instinctively inform your perception, decisions, and actions. The more you practice them, the less conscious attention they require of you. At some point they will then become habitual and integrated as a 'new you.' It is important to develop this Depth to ensure the Character remains part of your being. Without the prerequisite effort, they may remain superficial behaviours, easily forgotten. We take you on a journey through the 4Ls of Depth which habituate the Characters.

- **Learn: To comprehend the Character fully.** To understand its skills, assets and language. To know each Character, when to deploy it and how it should perform. At this stage, you may still need to be attentive and mindful of the need, but atleast you are aware of what, how, when and where the Character is used. At this Depth level, you are engaging through the **mind**.

- **Love: This is the passion and joy in the engagement of the Character.** Not just an eagerness in yourself but a desire to see it being practised around you. It inclines you towards putting the Character into play. It is the internal driver and motivator for you to put your awareness (Learn) into action. It provides a sense of flow and ease in your effort. At this Depth level, you are engaging feeling, through the **heart**.

- **Lead: Putting the knowledge into practice.** Having developed the skills necessary for the Character and the capacity to use it, you are able to deploy the Character as needed. At this Depth level, you are actively doing, engaging through the **body**.

- **Live: Embodying the Character fully so that it has become a habit.** You no longer need to actively think about the Character. You instinctively recognise the need and 'live' the Character. At this Depth level, you are becoming the Character, engaging through the **spirit**.

We shall examine the Characters in their respective Domains, that of Self, Others or Context. This allows us to explore the differences and similarities of each Character based on their environment. We then provide insight into their relationship with the other Characters in the same Dimension; how they complement, support and encourage each other.

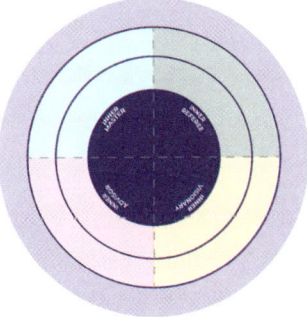

Characters in the Domain of Self

INNER MASTER

Inner Master resides in the Domain of Self and the Dimension of Understanding.

Who?

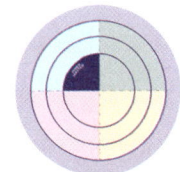

It is that part of self that is confident, resilient and aware of personal talents and personal challenges. Inner Master knows, accepts and understands what makes up personal identity, such as personal history, experiences, values, personality, culture, and context. Inner Master is like the database and processor of the self, recording experiences and memories  and allowing the emergence of identity and attributes answering the question 'who am I?' Inner Master is self-accepting, full of self-esteem and grounded. Inner Master trusts in the first line of the Serenity Prayer:

> *"God grant me the serenity to accept the things I cannot change."*

Inner Master accepts these facts about themselves, without recourse to judging, complaining, or boasting about them. Inner Master will, however, recognise areas for improvement and work towards becoming the best version of themselves. Inner Master's leadership role is to maintain peaceful resilience in the self, providing a deep-seated sense of identity and belonging.

Say and Do?

Motto: *'I know who I am'*

Inner Master understands the parameters and limitations of personal control and what is within its sphere of influence. Inner Master observes the self and probes to encourage a depth of self-awareness. You may hear Inner Master in phrases such as 'Let me find out about that', 'What does this say about me?' and 'Let me take a moment to reflect on that, and I'll get back to you'. Inner Master seeks first to know oneself before seeking an excuse or blame. Inner Master projects calmness and solidity.

Inner Master would not fumble its way through that which it does not know about. Inner Master is self-aware, and this self-awareness creates emotional self-regulation; so Inner Master provides the foundation for being emotionally intelligent and secure. The Inner Master has an internal locus of control and looks to manage and take responsibility for the situations it finds itself in.

Portrait

Dag Hammarskjold UN Secretary General 1953-1961, kept a personal diary that was published after his untimely death in a plane crash. The book is called 'Markings' and is a meditative and poetic insight into an exceptional leader's Inner Master. It shows Dag Hammarskjold as reflective, questioning, doubting and self-regulating of his thoughts and feelings and as a man who was committed at the core to authenticity in his leadership. He says:

> *"Our work for peace must begin within the private world of each one of us. To build for man a world without fear, we must be without fear. To build a world of justice, we must be just. And how can we fight for liberty if we are not free in our own minds?"*
> **(UN press release 22 December 1953)**

Theatre and film can also provide examples and clues to explore different Leadership Characters. The stories we tell in society are often a reflection of the thinking in that society. As such, there is no surprise that you can identify features of different Characters in protagonists and antagonists. Shakespeare's plays, for example, often have central characters who are people of influence or in leadership positions, such as kings, queens, princes, dukes, emperors, noble women and statesmen. Thus they can provide illustrations of Leadership Characters too. In the play, Hamlet, we find the Characters of the Understanding Dimension particularly stand out. Hamlet, the Prince of Denmark, explores his Inner Master with the audience in the soliloquy:

> *To be, or not to be: that is the question: Whether 'tis nobler in the mind to suffer the slings and arrows of outrageous fortune, or to take arms against a sea of troubles, and by opposing end them? To die: to sleep; no more; and by a sleep to say we end the heartache and the thousand natural shocks that flesh is heir to.*

Hamlet is trying to make sense of the situation he finds himself in. His loyalty to his dead father, his complicated feelings towards his mother and his conflict with his uncle, who is now his stepfather, whom he believes was the cause of his father's death. Hamlet becomes more and more self-aware as the play progresses. He reflects through a series of confidential exchanges with the audience to grow his Inner Master, which, once developed, propels him towards action and challenging the obstacles his uncle puts in his way.

Many more contemporary stories and writings of transformation or 'coming of age' involve the development of Inner Master too. In the book and film 'Divergent,' the character Beatrice Prior (Trish), lives in a sectarian world where belonging depends upon personality, inner talents, strengths and values. Trish goes against her family clan in her effort to understand and be true to herself. She senses that she does not fit (completely) into any one of these clans. As the story unfolds, she becomes aware that she belongs to nowhere and to everywhere; and more importantly, the Understanding of her uniqueness gives her strength and confidence, providing her with the courage to challenge norms that make others suffer.

See: Divergent in Good Leadership Book Movie Clips at:
https://www.youtube.com/c/goodleadership/playlists

Inner Master and Leadership

The journey of developing one's Inner Master is liberating. The enquiry opens awareness of talents, biases, preferences, cultural constructs, influencing forces from family and embodied responses to past experiences. Liberation and insight can be found in every act of self-awareness.

Knowing one's personal talents and abilities, accepting these as strengths that can be honed and offered in service to the world is a focused way to approach choices around roles and opportunities in life. Accepting what is mine to do, what is mine to learn, and what is better left for another. This insight also requires the humility to accept aspects of ourselves that have feelings of guilt and shame attached. Those parts of ourselves that we prefer to keep hidden, sometimes even from the self. These might include family expectations, feelings of personal failure or shame at having been born into a life upon which society projects low esteem. If we want to do something about the hidden aspects so that they don't emerge as shadows in our leadership, we must first accept them as part of reality. Acceptance is the first step to being able to make changes. This combination of self-awareness and self-acceptance builds a healthy self-esteem. Responsibility for who I am and who I want to become is located within the power of the individual.

A developed Inner Master creates a strong foundation for leaders to be aware of their 'red buttons' and work with them. Every person has flash points and vulnerabilities. Without self-awareness, a leader may 'act out' personal needs or unfulfilled aspects of psychological and emotional development in their leadership towards others. Of course, understanding self is never a one-off pursuit. We have blind spots about ourselves until a situation, a meditation or another person helps to bring them to light. An alert Inner Master, therefore, welcomes new opportunities to become aware of hidden aspects of the self and reduce blind spots to effective leadership. Tools for doing this include receiving feedback through structured interventions such as formal appraisals or by having a coach. Create a daily practice of noticing the world around you and your place in it.

Become a reflective observer of what opportunities and people are manifesting in your life and ask yourself: 'What is this situation presenting to me?' 'How do I feel?' 'How did I get here?' 'What do I need to learn from it?' The Inner Master is probably most efficiently developed through seeing a true reflection in the mirrors held to the self, often by others. This may not always feel comfortable, but the Inner Master is concerned with truthful awareness, and uncomfortable realisations are ultimately welcomed as opportunities to see and Understand more clearly.

Growing Up as Inner Master

Grow your Inner Master through exploring your inner self. Ask yourself why you think, feel and behave as you do. Psychometric and reflective tools can assist in raising questions and revealing answers. Consider your strengths and weaknesses. What motivates you or triggers certain emotions? On what paradigms do you rely for decision making? Whose opinions are you open to and whose repel you and why? How do stress, tiredness or pressure affect your performance? Develop an appetite for 'getting to know yourself' deeper. The more you learn, the more you will then regulate yourself based on your learning. Your current behaviours adapt, and you adopt new ones. Over time, these new behaviours become new habits.

The mature Inner Master has Depth in their Character. This is achieved through the 4Ls of development: Learn, Love, Lead and Live. Assess your Inner Master through reflecting on the statements in the table.

Score yourself based on:		
1 = Never; 2 = Sometimes; 3 = Most of the time; 4 = Always		
LEARN	*I understand my personal frames of reference*	
LOVE	*I accept and care for myself*	
LEAD	*I am present and self-aware*	
LIVE	*I am confident and comfortable with my identity*	

If you score 2 or below on any of the above, this is an area of development for you. Reflect using the guides below:

- **Learn: Have a good Understanding of your personal frames of reference.** Reflect on your life experiences and how they have shaped who you are. Focus on the 'here and now'. What thoughts, feelings and sensations arise in you? What might these be telling you about yourself and your 'window on the world'. Be present to what is real for you rather than what you would like it to be. Inner Master is about acknowledgment and self-awareness; about knowing who you are.

- **Love: Accept and care for yourself.** Appreciate your achievements. Consider how they make you feel proud. Reflect on what it is about you that helped you achieve these. Recognise who else has helped you achieve and nurture those relationships. Acknowledge and accept the things that have not gone as well as you would have liked.

- **Lead: Be present and self-aware.** Leverage your strengths. Master unproductive behaviours by seeking to understand and manage the emotions attached to them. Slow down. Take time to ensure thought, feeling and action are aligned.

- **Live: Being Confident and Comfortable with your own identity.** Seek regular and genuine feedback to inform your thinking. Know yourself, love yourself, be yourself, build yourself. Be in control of your responses - in the words of Viktor Frankl:

"The only thing you cannot take away from me is the way I respond to what you do to me."

A tool for exploring Inner Master: Conceptual Mapping:

1. Take a piece of paper and a pen.
2. Draw a circle and place your name in the centre.
3. Around the outside of the circle, write a list of experiences and identities that colour the way you see the world.

4. Reflect on your map. How has it helped you in the past? What does it help you see? What perspectives does it stop you from seeing? Who influenced your map? Is it a map that is still relevant for the future?

More tools are available in The Good Leadership Development Programme at www.goodleadership.org.

Summary

Inner Master gives you a positive sense of personal identity and confidence. Its key role is self-regulation. It manifests through the self-awareness of thoughts and feelings and the self-management of response and behaviour.

Knowing about Inner Master provides you with a cognizance that you see the world through your own personal frames of reference and that others must also have their frames of reference too. Inner Master allows you to connect to an authentic self that is confident and comfortable in its own skin. From this authentic position, it is possible to embark on self-leadership as a personal journey of deep Understanding, compassion and acceptance. Inner Master collaborates with the other three Inner Domain Characters (see later) in the following ways:

- The Inner Master gives the Inner Advisor the Understanding it needs to advise with a fuller insight.
- The Inner Master gives the Inner Referee insight into the effect of Ethical decisions on other areas of the self.
- The Inner Master gives the Inner Visionary deeper awareness of where you are at the start of the journey. It highlights strengths, challenges, and preferences. This allows the Inner Visionary to check out if the direction is 'right for me' based on fuller information.

INNER REFEREE

Inner Referee resides in the Domain of Self and the Dimension of Ethics.

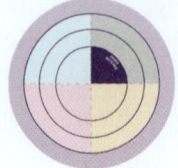

Who?

It is an accurate moral compass that moderates right action based upon alignment to important personal values. Inner Referee is the 'go to' Character for fairness and awareness of what is right and wrong in any situation.

Inner Referee is the twin of Inner Master in that they work best as a team. If Inner Master is all about self-awareness, then Inner Referee is about making choices from a moral perspective. It is the voice of personal conscience. Moral maturity requires development beyond moral reference points that come from family, society or are simply concerned with notions of reward and punishment. For example, when we learn from our parents or at school that it is wrong to take things that belong to other people, we also learn that we will be punished if we do so. We learn that bullying in the school playground will result in retribution, whether that is instigated by teachers or other children. This approach to what is right and wrong can sometimes be reduced to a moral code of 'will I be caught out?' In our adult world, where we are called upon to be morally responsible in our actions towards others, these lower levels of moral maturity cause huge problems for business and society. Witness the Barings bank collapse in 1995 as an example of a whole system being impacted by the immature moral conscience. Conversely, higher morals create stability, security, and communal responsibility. A mature Inner Referee provides the anchoring values for these higher levels of morality.

Inner Referee will also consider the diversity of value systems before making an Ethical decision. Its leadership role is to provide consistency in acting in a principled and fair way.

Say and Do?

Motto: *'This is my truth'*

Inner Referee does what is right, just and fair. It would ask, 'What is the right thing to do?' It does not matter to Inner Referee who is watching in order to act according to core values and principles. Many of these principles can be universally held; however, Inner Referee gives each weight depending on its own level of maturity. For example, Inner Referee may need to choose between:

1. Personal benefit: the extent to which an action produces beneficial consequences for the individual in question.
2. Social benefit: the extent to which an action produces beneficial consequences for society.
3. Benevolence: helping those in need.
4. Paternalism: assisting others in pursuing their best interests.
5. Harm: do not harm others.
6. Honesty: do not deceive others.
7. Lawfulness: do not violate the law.
8. Justice: acknowledging a person's right to due process, fair compensation for harm done, and fair distribution of benefits.
9. Rights: a person's rights to life, information, privacy, free expression, and safety.

The Inner Referee may be called upon to help make difficult decisions, and sometimes the 'lesser of two evils.' What if honesty leads to harm; justice requires the violation of law; or societal benefit can be gained by the breach of another's rights? A mature Inner Referee uses its strongly held values as touchstones in such cases.

Portrait

Inner Referee fosters inner peace, and therefore, actions that go against Inner Referee create disharmony and a moral 'itch.' Dr. Maya Anjelou puts this succinctly:

> *"I belong to myself. I'm very proud of that. I am very concerned about how I look at Maya. I like Maya very much. I like the humour and courage very much. And When I find myself acting in a way that isn't...that doesn't please me then I have to deal with that."*

Inner Referee makes us accountable firstly to ourselves at the deepest possible level. When Inner Referee works collaboratively with Inner Master, lessons in trust, equality and justice can be had in ways that increase a positive sense of self and makes it possible to look at personal moral failures straight on, deal with them and learn from them. Together, the talent they bring is one of discernment. Inner Referee is the Character that provides the standard for the Inner Master to become aware of inner moral transgressions and provides the direction for the Inner Master to take actions to bring about an improved state of personal balance and harmony.

In Shakespeare's A Winter's Tale, Paulina, a noblewoman relies on her Inner Referee to know what is right and speak truth. She is confident in her moral position and highlights the shortcomings of others who fail to tell Leontes, the King, the unpalatable truth that he has wrongly accused his wife of being unfaithful:

> *I come to bring him sleep. 'Tis such as you, that creep like shadows by him, and do sigh at each his needless heavings; such as you nourish the cause of his awaking. I do come with words as medicinal as true, honest, as either...*

She is a highly moral woman willing to risk her life for what she believes is right. Paulina's values drive her to mediate for sixteen years between Leontes and his supposed dead wife Hermione, until such time as he is ready to accept his mistakes and seek forgiveness. Paulina challenges Leontes, using her Inner Referee to give her both guidance and confidence.

Contemporary films that highlight the role of Inner Referee include 'Seven Pounds.' The central character Ben Thomas feels passionately that he must make amends for a historic mistake. He seeks out seven people in need and is driven by his personal value of justice and conscience to enhance their lives, even though it meant losing his own.

> See: Seven Pounds in Good Leadership Book Movie Clips at:
> https://www.youtube.com/c/goodleadership/playlists

In the Marvel film 'Captain America, Civil War,' Captain Rodgers is compelled by his personal values to retain loyalty to his friend ("I'm with you till the end of the line"), personal responsibility ("if I see a situation pointing south, I cannot ignore it") and not to surrender power to external politically driven leaders ("I know we are not perfect, but the safest hands are still our own"). Iron Man is driven by his newly acquired personal values of oversight and governance following the death of innocent people and the need to right the wrong of his parents' death. Black Panther shows remarkable discernment, combining both the Inner Referee and the Inner Master, when he confesses, "vengeance has consumed you; it is consuming them; I am done letting it consume me." A clash of beliefs and values held by individual characters leads to 'civil war' between the heroes. Deeply held Inner Referee core values can become a source of conflict with others who hold core values that may be different or with those who may stand in the way of yours.

> See: Marvel's Captain America:
> Civil War in Good Leadership Book Movie Clips at:
> https://www.youtube.com/c/goodleadership/playlists

Inner Referee and Leadership

Again, Dag Hammarskjold gives a clear insight into the significant role of Inner Referee in leadership:

> *"A mature man is his own judge. In the end, his only firm support is being faithful to his own convictions. The advice of others may be welcome and valuable, but it does not free him from responsibility."*

Inner Referee gives a leader the authority upon which they can take personal responsibility for decisions and actions. It moderates biases in deciphering right from wrong. It ensures interventions are positive and fair. It encourages humility, honesty and forgiveness. A developed Inner Referee gives stability and consistency to a leader's actions. It allows a leader to be steadfast and resistant to outside pressures whilst maintaining transparency and fair-mindedness in considering the viewpoints of others.

Growing Up as Inner Referee

Grow your Inner Referee through exploring Ethical and moral challenges. Seek out stories that present Ethical challenges, such as the play 'Enron' by Lucy Prebble and the film 'Eye in the Sky.' These scenarios can help test your moral compass and get you to review the strength of your beliefs. They will make you aware of the standards that you rely upon whilst making judgments. The pursuit will inspire you to apply your lens on more complex or abstract problems over time. You will learn about your red lines, the boundaries you are willing to stretch and the rules you are willing to break. Over time, you will become more familiar with the consequences of both rigidity and flexibility in your values.

The mature Inner Referee will have Depth in their Character. This is achieved through the 4Ls of development: Learn, Love, Lead and Live. Assess your Inner Referee through reflecting on the statements in the table.

Score yourself based on:		
1 = Never; 2 = Sometimes; 3 = Most of the time; 4 = Always		
LEARN	*I have a good understanding of my personal values*	
LOVE	*I am content and motivated with my moral position*	
LEAD	*I am an ethical role model and walk the talk*	
LIVE	*I am authentic and have high integrity*	

If you score 2 or below on any of the above, this is an area of development for you. Reflect using the guides below:

- **Learn: Have a good grasp of your personal values.** Reflect on your life choice using the lens of morality. Consider why you believe what you do. How do you feel when you see or hear about unethical behaviour? Read about varying Ethical viewpoints, from Aristotle to religious frameworks to present day paradigms. What rings 'true' to you?

- **Love: Be content and uplifted with your moral position.** Know your principles hold great value. Be gentle on yourself with lapses of judgement. Be glad to be right, whilst accepting that there can be more than one right.
- **Lead: Be an Ethical role model, walk the talk and be steadfast.** Wear your values on your sleeve. Be transparent and honest about who you are. Be aware of your conduct and strive to be the best example. Give and take 'good' advice regularly. Set standards through personal conduct. Measure your actions against the highest standards.
- **Live: Be authentic and have high integrity.** Good begets good, keep the company of 'good' people. Know what you believe and be true to it. Continually strive to build your character and live with a 'heart at peace.'

A tool for exploring Inner Referee: My Values:

1. Take six sticky notes.
2. On each, write one value you hold dear. Consider those values you feel are non-negotiable. Remember, you bring the 'value to your values.' So be subjective. Try not to think too deeply at this stage; often your first thought is the right one. Examples could include justice, professionalism, equality, family, honesty, fun, humility etc. Use your own words and don't worry about the technicalities of the definition.
3. Consider each value. Why do you hold it so dearly?
4. Now select one value that is the least valuable from the set. If you had to discard it to protect the others, which one would you sacrifice? Take this sticky note and set it aside.
5. Repeat this again, but with the five remaining values. If you had to sacrifice one to protect the others, which would it be? Set this aside too under the previously removed value.
6. Repeat this activity until you are left with only one sticky note.
7. Consider: What did the process of discarding values feel like? Was it easy or hard? What does this tell you about yourself or the value? What order did you remove the values? What does this tell

you about yourself? What is your remaining value? If this is so important, then how do you live this value and wear it on your sleeve?

The exercise can be done keeping in mind either the values 'you live by' or the values you 'aspire to live by.' Ensure you do not mix them. However, the exercise can be repeated using the other set of values once complete.

More tools are available in The Good Leadership Development Programme at www.goodleadership.org.

Summary

Inner Referee knows the principles upon which decisions about the rightness of an action are predicated and is willing to override lower orders of moral thinking, such as 'what's in it for me' for higher levels that embrace the broader moral issues of social contract and universalism.

Inner Referee's key role is self-decency and uprightness. To ensure your actions 'do no harm' and 'spread goodness.' Inner Referee collaborates with the other three Inner Domain Characters in the following ways:

- The Inner Referee gives the Inner Advisor the steer to ensure self-talk remains aligned to values.
- The Inner Referee gives the Inner Master its conscience.
- The Inner Referee gives the Inner Visionary a measure of the correctness of its direction.

INNER VISIONARY

Inner Visionary resides in the Domain of Self and the Dimension of Purpose.

Who?

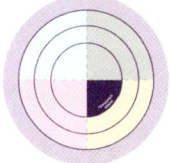

It tugs the heart towards a clear target; points out the goal that you desire to reach. If Inner Referee is about the rightness of a direction, then Inner Visionary illuminates the direction and destination you are traveling. Inner Visionary answers the question: 'What is my reason for being?' It is deeply connected to what inspires and lights up an individual internally and helps manifest the unique Purpose of every individual.

Inner Visionary is a highly intuitive Character. It is energetic, motivating, passionate, adaptive, joyful, focused, and future orientated. Its leadership role is as an inspirer and a positive force for fulfilling human potential.

Say and Do?

Motto: *'I know what I want'*

Knowing Inner Visionary is the same as knowing your personal Purpose. It connects time past and time future in time present. Inner Visionary builds partnerships and seeks out travel companions that can help reach its destination. It is the drive behind meaningful actions. Inner Visionary dares to step out beyond boundaries and tests limits. Inner Visionary explores 'what can be' and then inspires, articulates, and determines meaning from it. Inner Visionary says, 'this is my path, let's go' and always keeps us on that path. Inner Visionary embraces change and enjoys the journey. If Inner Master and Inner Referee help you become the best version of your current self, then Inner Visionary motivates you to be 'all that you can be.' Inner Visionary would find the value in the effort and uses experience to inform the future.

Portrait

When Inner Visionary is alive within an individual, it provides an abundant source of ideas and energy in the pursuit of goals to which it is aligned. Inner Visionary powerfully connects your heart's desire with tangible action and motion. It encourages dreaming bigger and inspires living the dream. The German playwright Johann Wolfgang von Goethe said:

> *"Whatever you can do or dream you can, begin it. Boldness has genius, power, and magic in it."*

In Shakespeare's play, Macbeth's Inner Visionary is ignited by the prophecy of the three witches. They foresee him becoming the thane (lord) of Cawdor, Glamis and thereafter, the King of Scotland. When he hears that King Duncan is giving him the title of thane of Cawdor, he begins to muse on what might be the path to his goal to become King:

> *This supernatural soliciting cannot be ill; cannot be good. If ill, why hath it given me earnest of success, commencing in a truth? I am thane of Cawdor*

The seed for the murder of Duncan is sown. Although acting with the insights of the Inner Visionary, it is noteworthy to remember that, without the Inner Referee ensuring the correctness of direction, Macbeth's Purpose is not a righteous one.

A film to see Inner Visionary in action is the 2016 movie called 'Joy'. The protagonist has a vision and a personal Purpose that she is not going to be limited by perceptions, barriers, or false realities. She knows what she wants and works hard to keep her vision clear in her mind.

> See: Joy in Good Leadership Book Movie Clips at:
> https://www.youtube.com/c/goodleadership/playlists

Music is also a place to find expressions of Inner Visionary, taking you to places in your imagination, stimulating senses and speaking so eloquently to the yearnings of the heart. Listen to your favourite lyrics and music; pay attention to where your Inner Visionary goes.

The musician Stevie Wonder, blind from childhood, wrote the song 'Visions' on the album 'Inner Visions' in which he describes a world where hate is a thing of the past and all men are truly free. Likewise, John Lennon's song 'Imagine' invites you to use Inner Visionary to see a world where people are all living in peace. All images of the future, inviting your Inner Visionary to be influenced.

Inner Visionary and Leadership

Leadership creates pathways to a desirable future. It sees from a future reality, a vision in our minds lighting the way and aligning personal Purpose to action. Inner Visionary discerns where you want to be in your life five years or ten years from now, or even at the end of your life and helps set the direction of your efforts.

Purpose enables human beings to connect to future possibilities by imagining what is yet to come. For this, being a creative and innovative thinker is important. Having clarity of personal destination provides motivation and tenacity to keep moving forward, even in adversity. It inspires optimism and optimal performance. It helps drive you beyond basic survival and opens up possibilities, collaborations and strategic leaps. It provides certainty even in uncharted terrains and new pathways.

Growing Up as Inner Visionary

Growing the Inner Visionary requires curiosity. Notice synchronicity, a coincidence of unconnected events with a related or common meaning. Do they show where the energy is flowing in your life? Follow that as a golden thread. Listen to your dreams and their symbols. Find all the elements that connect you to a sense of joyful optimism about your future. Be alive to that which is energising in your life and what tugs at your heart. Notice words and phrases that leap out and inspire you. Observe your 'choiceless choices', the things you feel compelled to do because of the person you have become. Give your awareness a clear language that inspires action and allows you to share your new direction. Act with boldness to do the things you must do and notice the things you need not do because they are not yours to actually do. Over time, you get clarity on your raison d'etre.

The mature Inner Visionary will have Depth in their Character. This is achieved through the 4Ls of development: Learn, Love, Lead and Live. Assess your Inner Visionary through reflecting on the statements in the table.

Score yourself based on:		
1 = Never; 2 = Sometimes; 3 = Most of the time; 4 = Always		
LEARN	*I have conscious intentions and plans for life's journey*	
LOVE	*I have a joy in engaging in life's journey*	
LEAD	*I am brave in experiencing what is new and stepping into the unknown*	
LIVE	*I am driven, determined and focused*	

If you score 2 or below on any of the above, this is an area of development for you. Reflect using the guides below:

- **Learn: Have conscious intentions and plans for life's journey.** Focus on the future and get to know what you need to do in life and work. Commit yourself to a course of action. Ask yourself: how will you know when you are on your path? If you woke up tomorrow and your vision of your future was here already, what would be different? What does it look like? Who else is there? What are you saying and doing? Inner Visionary is about knowing where you are heading and what to do to get there.

- **Love: Have joy in engaging with your journey.** Be enthused about your direction. Be inspired and motivated even during setbacks. Know you are moving forward and that both the journey and the destination are fulfilling.

- **Lead: Be brave in experiencing what is new and stepping into the unknown.** Have clarity in direction and articulate it well to others. Walk the talk. Ensure you are moving forward every day. Build a vision community to assist you in getting to where you need to go. Create milestones and plans and ensure you are measuring progress regularly.

- **Live: Be driven and determined.** Success breeds success - keep building on your accomplishments. Be certain of direction and strive to reach there constantly. Be inspired and inspiring. Motivated and motivating. Focused and focusing.

A tool for exploring Inner Visionary: Vision Drawing:

1. You will need a blank sheet of paper and coloured pens.
2. Draw your vision of the future 5 years from now.
3. What are the images that symbolise success?
4. Try not to draw a series of 'achievements,' e.g., a car, an office, a family - ask yourself 'why?' to all those things and draw the answer to that question.
5. Once you have your imagery describe it in words and note the pertinent words down.
6. Use these words that have emerged from your 'image of a successful future' to craft yourself a vision statement.

More tools are available in The Good Leadership Development Programme at www.goodleadership.org.

Summary

Inner Visionary is like the pin on a map; the bull's eye of a target, highlighting the road to be travelled. Inner Visionary gives you meaning. Its key role is self-motivation towards a clear Purpose in life. It allows you to step outside your frames of reference and allows imagination and innovation to thrive. It pushes you outside of your comfort zone and brings passion and possibilities to your leadership journey. Inner Visionary collaborates with the other three Inner Domain Characters in the following ways:

- Inner Visionary gives the Inner Advisor a reference point to ensure it keeps in mind the direction of travel.
- Inner Visionary gives Inner Master insights into personal desire and extrinsic motivation. It allows Inner Master to apply its assets to moving forward where uncertainty exists.
- Inner Visionary will often give Inner Referee a challenge. It will push towards a less trodden road and force Inner Referee to assess potential consequences.

INNER ADVISOR

Inner Advisor resides in the Domain of Self and the Dimension of Communication.

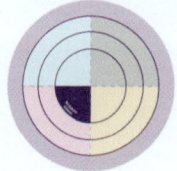

Who?

It is the inner voice that knows the power of the pause button and the power of speaking out. It is the way you Communicate with self. A trustworthy friend to turn to at times for advice if we stop and listen. Tuning into the voice of Inner Advisor will reveal its wisdom. It does not hold back unless you mute it yourself. A well-developed Inner Advisor is  a critical, honest best friend, telling you what you 'need' to hear or, when not developed properly, a mischievous whisperer, skilled in the art of self-deception, giving you only what you 'want' to hear.

Sometimes our inner Communication can be a noisy affair. Inner Referee is saying, 'don't do that, it's not the right thing'; Inner Master is saying, 'my needs have been overlooked for years and now is the time to take a stand'; Inner Visionary is saying, 'the world isn't ready for this yet.' Compound this with the advent of social media platforms like Instagram, WhatsApp, Twitter (X), Snapchat, and Facebook. These platforms further take socialising away from the need to physically be present with another and 'speak out loud,' and thus, human beings are socialising internally with themselves, overloading with information, much from unreliable sources. Inner Advisor thus needs to have a clear and compelling voice so that you stop and attend to it. You question, it answers, it questions, you answer. You need to listen for its influences, is it relaying the wishes of the Inner Visionary, Inner Referee, Inner Master, or someone else? To hear the wisdom of Inner Advisor, you must remain open to what it raises, it will always speak to you. It is, however, up to you to stop and pay attention. Its leadership role is as the mouthpiece of the other Characters of the Inner Domain.

Say and Do?

Motto: *'I can help'*

Inner Advisor provides self-talk and encouragement. It responds to the question: 'What does this mean?' Providing answers to questions that arise as one contemplates and meditates. Inner Advisors ensures 'the self' has a voice. It is the gateway and enabler for self-awareness, self-regulation, and self-exploration.

Portrait

A developed Inner Advisor is an inner adult voice. The therapeutic model of Transactional Analysis describes there being a Parent, Adult and Child inner voice in everyone. The inner parental voice can be critical or nurturing, and the inner child voice can be rebellious or compliant. When parental or child inner voices are activated in either their positive or negative guises, they detract from the person connecting to a mature adult version of themselves. In this way, we can say that a mature Inner Advisor is like the adult voice in the Transactional Analysis model. It is calming, centred, aware of the noise of the other voices but not drawn into them.

In Shakespeare's Richard III, the leadership journey of Richard begins with his own self-loathing. His Inner Advisor provides answers that lead to a personal transformation from 'self-disgust' to 'dangerous to know.' He begins:

> *But I, that am not shap'd for sportive tricks, nor made to court an amorous looking glass; I, that am rudely stamp'd, and want love's majesty to strut before a wanton ambling nymph; I, that am curtail'd of this fair proportion, cheated of feature by dissembling nature, deform'd, unfinish'd, sent before my time into this breathing world, scarce half made up, and that so lamely and unfashionable that dogs bark at me as I halt by them.*

But to keep the attention of Lady Anne, who has taken an interest in him, he reflects:

> *Upon my life, she finds, although I cannot, myself to be a marv'lous proper man. I'll be at charges for a looking glass and entertain a score or two of tailors to study*

fashions to adorn my body. Since I am crept in favor with myself, I will maintain it with some little cost.

He listens and acts upon Inner Advisor's messages which stimulate his transformation. He does, however, ignore his Inner Referee which ultimately leads to the failure of his leadership.

A contemporary film to watch Inner Advisor in action is 13 Days. President Kennedy must manage a critical situation, the Cuban Missile Crisis, which could escalate into World War 3. Although the film is as much about him having a range of external advisors, a full suite of them, he is tuned to his own Inner Advisor too. His instinct and what he feels is right or wrong. He listens to the voice in his head (and heart), discounting prejudice, bias, and knee jerk reactions. His Inner Advisor stops him from making rash decisions, and he ensures his reflections are his own voices, taking time to consider the range of opinions of his external advisors, but not abdicating his own responsibility and accountability through blindly following them.

See: Thirteen Days in Good Leadership Book Movie Clips at:
https://www.youtube.com/c/goodleadership/playlists

Inner Advisor and Leadership

'Putting the pause button on' was a technique that was shared at a leadership programme with a young man in his twenties whose life was chaotic. He had significant anxiety issues, panic disorder and a diagnosis of bipolar disorder. He had little insight into his condition and said he was attending the programme to learn how to 'manipulate others' more effectively, possibly an externalised desire to get control of his own life. We sat until the early hours of the morning, discussing possibilities for his life to come into a greater sense of balance. Two years later, he related the changes in his life: *"I saw a 100% rise in my business in a year. I am not losing friends anymore; I feel at peace, I am not fighting myself anymore; when I am having problems, I can talk about my issues with the other person rather than cutting the relationship."* When asked what he does when he finds himself feeling some of the intense feelings that previously used to take over his life in a destructive way, his reply was that he goes to the beach, sits and looks out to the horizon and takes a pause. *"I am not 100% cured but for 90% of the time when I am going through a phase, I can say this is because of my mental conditions and I try to control those emotions."*

This young man's life has changed because he found a way to connect to his Inner Advisor and use it to support Inner Master.

A journey of growth often starts with an Inner Advisor creating a still enough place internally to bring things back to a state of equilibrium and balance. Without it, our inner systems are noisy, anxious, and reactive to over stimulation from our environment. We all need to find our own pause button. All leadership journeys start with an active Inner Advisor, the inner voice that is capable of gently steering inner focus away from distracting inner chatter and towards a stronger sense of expressing a truthful, authentic voice.

Growing Up as Inner Advisor

Growing the Inner Advisor requires stillness and time to be heard. Notice the voice in your head and what it is saying. What is the distraction of your mind? Where are your thoughts? When do you shut your own inner voice down? What does it advise that is kind? When is it self-justifying? Does it speak to you from the head or the heart? Does it repeat the thoughts of others or develop its own thinking? Which of the other Dimensions gets the most bandwidth from your inner voice? Which is most neglected? Over time, you become more attuned to yourself. Think about the positive things you do that help you connect with your Inner Advisor and make your stress level feel less like it has reached tipping point. Gardening, walking, praying, dancing, cooking, painting can all be helpful activities that bring us to a better sense of balance. Listen to your Inner Advisor as one would listen to a compassionate and trusted friend.

The mature Inner Advisor will have Depth in their Character. This is achieved through the 4Ls of development: Learn, Love, Lead and Live. Assess your Inner Master through reflecting on the statements in the table.

Score yourself based on:		
1 = Never; 2 = Sometimes; 3 = Most of the time; 4 = Always		
LEARN	*I recognise and understand my inner voices*	
LOVE	*I am centred*	
LEAD	*I am able to reflect well*	
LIVE	*I am completely tuned in to self*	

If you score 2 or below on any of the above, this is an area of development for you. Reflect using the guides below:

- **Learn: Recognise and understand your inner voices.** Put a pause button on your 'busyness.' Tune in to yourself as a regular practice of prayer, contemplation, or meditation. Even 10 minutes every day helps still the inner chatter and get close to the true self. Pay attention to the red flags and your instincts. Decipher the language of the Inner Advisor; When is it being urgent? When is it being persistent? When is it compassionate? When is it giving you a warning?

- **Love: Be centred.** Enjoy self-talk. Take pleasure in the emergence after reflection. Recognise yourself as the most important advisor of self!

- **Lead: Reflect well.** Constantly take time out to notice the inner voice. Do not allow it to be silenced by the pressures of everyday living. Give your inner voice unrestricted access to Understanding, Ethics and Purpose Dimensions.

- **Live: Be completely tuned in to self.** You have found your voice. Be mindfully present. Be still and notice all the sensations and messages the body gives you.

A tool for exploring Inner Advisor: Mindfulness:

There are many exercises for Mindfulness to try. This one can be done alone but is better shared with a friend or coach.

1. Think of one thing that may be stressing you and another that you are excited about.

2. Share them with a friend in detail. Describe the issue but also your thoughts, feelings, behaviours, and attitudes relating to them.
3. Reflect upon: What language are you using whilst describing each? How does the language differ between stressful and exciting events? What is the tone, pitch, and emphasis?
4. What are you feeling as you narrate or reflect on each? What are you thinking? What are your bodily sensations?
5. Where do you notice any mind wandering or distractions? How did you / do you remain focused?
6. What are the sources of your justifications for the behaviours and actions you have taken (or are considering taking) in response to each?

More tools are available in The Good Leadership Development Programme at www.goodleadership.org.

Summary

Inner Advisor is the adult inner voice that can provide critical, friendly feedback. When we know our Inner Advisor and listen to it, we can stay present in the reality of our situation. Its key role is self-reflection. Inner Advisor is both the pause button and play button on our inner dialogue. It gives a voice to other Inner Domain Characters and credibility or challenge to the voice of others. Inner Advisor collaborates with the other three Inner Domain Characters in the following ways:

- The Inner Advisor gives the Inner Master the tools to reflect and further strengthen the Understanding of Self.
- The Inner Advisor gives the Inner Referee the tools and time to reflect upon the correctness of situations it is presented with.
- The Inner Advisor gives the Inner Visionary opportunities to check out direction and reminders to keep going in both good and hard times.

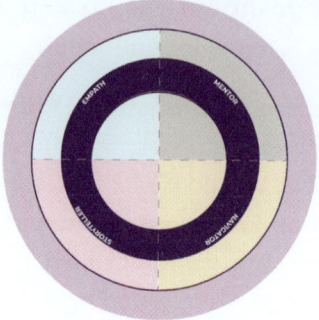

Characters in the Domain of Others

EMPATH

Empath resides in the Domain of Others and the Dimension of Understanding.

Who?

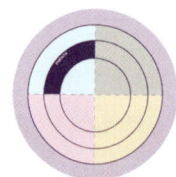

It comprehends a situation from the perspective of the other, putting itself in 'another's shoes.' It is a whole person connection with recognition of another's realities as valid and real. It extends beyond the intellectual, it is also felt in the body and experienced as a sensation of the heart. When your Empath is active, you will be aware of how another is feeling on the inside. Empath relates to another's humanity, aware of vulnerabilities and flaws, as well as positive traits. Empath enables others to feel understood and thus is central to occupations such as counselling.

Empath is genuinely interested in people and is curious about what makes a person who they are. It has a core talent for both listening and deduction. Empath builds rapport with another person, gets on their wavelength, and connects to them. It knows what is happening on the inside as much as outward behaviour. Empath is non-judgmental. Not an easy position to take; to both suspend judgment, whilst listening to be influenced, with an open heart. Empath is a Character who first seeks to understand the other before intervening. Its leadership role is to enable a deeper appreciation of others and so facilitates more effective solutions to be co-created.

Say and Do?

Motto: *'I understand you'*

Empath is all about identifying with another. It asks questions and listens attentively to get a fuller sense of things. It matches and mirrors body language and vocal tone in ways that let the other person know, 'I get you.' When called upon, Empath will be 'present' in another's distress and vulnerability, feeling and relating to it too. This makes Empath a true 'friend in need.' Empath doesn't offer minimising platitudes like 'don't worry, you'll be fine.' It says, 'I can see you are upset by this and I'm going to stay here with you. You are not alone.'

Empath builds trust by sharing difficult and dark places with others whilst celebrating successes with equal joy too.

Portrait

Models of Emotional Intelligence (EQ) include Self Awareness, Self-Management, Empathy and Managing Social Relationships. These are the Inner Master, and the Empath combined. Research shows that it is possible to enhance EQ and that it is more important than IQ for success. This is not surprising as EQ helps build strong social networks and relationships. In fact, schools that teach Emotional Intelligence even notice around a 30% increase in exam grades.

Empath in a line manager will make difficult conversations and motivating a team easier. It is central to Understanding others and taking an active interest in their concerns. Lack of empathy leads to people feeling isolated, ignored, and angry. People have bad days at work and at home. Noticing this in another person, asking how they feel and listening to their response is being Empath. And, as the saying goes, a problem shared is a problem halved. Motivated only to build an Understanding of the other, Empath's genuine interest is enough to lessen the emotional load another is carrying.

In Shakespeare's play, you see Hamlet's Empath in his Understanding of the feelings of Laertes, who has, like him, lost his father and now also his sister. At Ophelia's graveside Hamlet unexpectedly meets Laertes and they fight. Later, speaking to a trusted friend, Hamlet wants to apologise and move towards reconciliation.

But I am very sorry, good Horatio, that to Laertes I forgot myself. for by the image of my cause I see the portraiture of his. I'll court his favours.

In more contemporary stories, you can see Empath in action, in the TV series, The Mentalist. Patrick Jane, the central character, is very aware of others. What they are saying, what they are not saying, what they mean, and what they don't mean. He reads body language, tone and pitch. He observes intently the mannerisms of those he engages with. He relates to them and sees the world through their eyes to Understand and deduce innocence from guilt.

See: The Mentalist and The Mentalist 2.01 in Good Leadership Book Movie Clips at: https://www.youtube.com/c/goodleadership/playlists

Empath and Leadership

An engaging Empath can make a huge difference in situations where emotions are running high and there is something significant at stake. In leadership, these include situations that have been described as 'crucial conversations'. These are leadership dialogues that bring change, whether that is a call to action, a change in behaviour or a change in a relationship. A crucial conversation requires you to fully enter the dialogue and suspend personal judgment (or, at least, be aware of when personal judgments are in play). Empath makes the best effort to attend to what the other is communicating. Empathic Understanding is a game changer and a whole-body experience. We hear with our ears, but we also hear with our hearts. We can pick up subtleties in body language and sense what those signals might mean. Empath is very skilled at listening to the whole person: heart, mind, body, and spirit with their full range of senses. When Empath's acute perceptiveness engages, the other person feels understood.

An example of a situation in which Empath can help to shift a difficult dynamic is during conflict resolution. Appropriate mediation would invite someone to see from the other's perspective. To step into their shoes and experience what the situation is like from their worldview. When people see through another's eyes, they recognise that the other has specific needs too. When experiencing this, we move from the position of 'I win, so you must lose' to finding solutions that feel right for both parties. Empath enables us to go beyond our own needs and widen our gaze to include the needs of others.

Empath creates a safe space for Storyteller and Mentor (see later) to speak openly and truthfully. Empath is their close brother. In the Domain of Others, Empath forms a dynamic dialogue with each. It listens and they respond. It sees, hears, and empathises and they speak, write and guide based on this Understanding. Empath is also crucial to being able to change dominant narratives that perpetuate prejudice. It is the Character that opens our hearts and minds to seeing inequalities in society. It helps us to hear, see and thus respond, finding sustainable and respectful solutions to deeply entrenched social fault lines.

Growing Up as Empath

Your Empath grows as you learn about others. You develop an interest in knowing what makes others tick. You take joy in building relationships, which then become richer and more genuine. You take time to get to know people and are confident in letting them get to know you. Over time, this becomes more natural for you.

The mature Empath will have Depth in their Character. This is achieved through the 4Ls of development: Learn, Love, Lead and Live. Assess your Empath through reflecting on the statements in the table.

Score yourself based on:		
1 = Never; 2 = Sometimes; 3 = Most of the time; 4 = Always		
LEARN	*I understand the frames of reference of others*	
LOVE	*I am passionate about engaging with others*	
LEAD	*I am approachable and relate well with others*	
LIVE	*I am competent, confident and comfortable with other people*	

If you score 2 or below on any of the above, this is an area of development for you. Reflect using the guides below:

- **Learn: Develop a good Understanding of other's frames of reference.** Try looking through the window at the world of other people. Seek to know what others value in their relationships and what inspires their action. Accept what is real and true for them, even if it conflicts with your own worldview. Take time to appreciate their likes and dislikes. Explore another's motives, experiences and personality.

- **Love: Be passionate about engaging with others.** Accept and acknowledge them as people. Ask open questions and be curious and intrigued by the response. Be comfortable with allowing others to steer the conversation. Smile, laugh and share humour. Feel content knowing that you have listened to another and made them feel valued.

- **Lead: Be approachable and relate well to others.** Give people your time and ensure they feel heard. Reflect, repeat, or paraphrase comments and mirror behaviour. Actively listen and use gestures to emphasise this. Take an interest in them personally and professionally. Good questions could include: Tell me about your earliest childhood memory. What do you like/dislike about being part of this team? How was your weekend? How are you feeling? How was your working day? Are you struggling with any part of your work? Before starting meetings, take time to attune yourself to others.

- **Live: Be competent, confident, and comfortable with other people.** Be non-judgmental until another's view is fully explored. Be open to the influence of others. Embrace the diversity of thought, feeling, practice and culture around you. Look for commonalities whilst embracing differences. Influence through pacing and building rapport. Comfort begets comfort, allow others to feel at ease and build trust through your actions.

A tool for exploring Empath: Highs and Lows:

This activity can be done with family or work colleagues.

1. Assemble in a circle or around the table.
2. Each member takes turns to share the highlight and low points of the previous day or week.
3. After each member shares, spend 10 minutes asking open questions to better understand the situation.
4. Listen empathetically. Put yourself in their shoes. See the world through their eyes. Try and relate to the feelings and the reasons behind the feelings.
5. At the end of the activity, collectively share what may have surprised you, what you may have learned about yourself and others and how the experience will add to your empathy journey.

More tools are available in The Good Leadership Development Programme at www.goodleadership.org.

Relationship with the Inner Domain (Inner Master)

A developed Inner Master enables an Empath. Understanding yourself allows you to put aside 'what you know' to explore another's known world without prejudice. You need to be able to Understand what you are projecting onto others to see them as they truly are. However, Empath also acts as a mirror for Inner Master. In putting aside your own views and desires to empathically engage with others, how does this feel? What are you compromising? What is comfortable and uncomfortable to hear? Through reflection and with practice, you find yourself moving fluidly between stretching outwards and connecting back inwards. A metaphor for this is an elastic band that has the capability of both stretching to an expanded size and relaxing back into its original shape. This movement of stretching and relaxing between Domains is the pulse of growth. Through our empathic encounters, we connect to this pulse and grow.

Summary

Empath's key role is to holistically connect with others. It prioritises another over the self. It is the means of Understanding the world through the eyes of another. It allows you to, as the native American proverb says, 'never judge another until you have walked a mile in their moccasins.' In doing so, it provides diverse, meaningful, and insightful Understanding. It opens the opportunity to influence in a respectful and human way. It is the gateway Character to a mutually enhancing, dialogical engagement with others. Empath collaborates with the other three 'Domain of Others' Characters in the following ways:

- Empath gives Storyteller the Understanding it needs to make a stronger impact on others.
- Empath gives Mentor the insight into the effect of its Ethical direction on others. It provides feedback that Mentor can use to help inform its interventions.
- Empath gives Navigator an awareness of where people are in their life journey. It allows Navigator to relate to others and better share their experience, ambition, and motivation.

MENTOR

Mentor resides in the Domain of Others and the Dimension of Ethics.

Who?

It engages with others to enable their Ethical growth. Mentor is proactive in supporting another to become the best version of themselves. Its role is to keep that person heading in the correct moral direction. First and foremost, Mentor is person-focused rather than task-focused. This means that Mentor sees others as valuable individuals and not

as objects to be used as tools to achieve ends. Mentors are often formal or informal teachers in our lives. Whether linked to an educational institute or even a friend or work colleague. Its primary interest is the development of the mentee. Its leadership role is to help others become 'better people'.

Say and Do?

Motto: *'Be good'*

Mentor holds others to account for their actions. It makes sure they practice their espoused values. Mentor's role is to support the alignment of people to values that, in turn, develop a virtuous and ethical individual, organisation or society. It influences others in a positive way. It will highlight weaknesses and how behaviour can be out of alignment with core values. It will then support corrective action. Mentor will be present with the mentee as they achieve, struggle and fall. They enable the mentee to get back up and move their lives forward in a positive direction. In this way, Mentor is an effective companion of Empath. If Empath says, 'I get where you are coming from,' Mentor would say, 'and I can see that what you are doing is causing harm, let's try going about this in a different way.' In organisations like Alcoholics Anonymous, recovering addicts, have Mentors called sponsors, to help them maintain sobriety. Mentor sets a benchmark for accountability and makes sure others walk their talk. Alongside Empath in the team,

Mentor can provide a moral direction that is Understanding of the challenges and works to overcome them.

Portrait

Mentor is a helper and guide. It shares these qualities with Navigator too (see later). However, for Mentor, the motivation is to build another's character (unlike Navigator, which is concerned with achieving a goal). Mentor is a constant reminder and anchor for others. It provides the moral underpinning for the activities of the Empath, Navigator and Storyteller (see later). Mentor in a line manager will ensure that difficult conversations are had. It is central to ensuring people 'do the right thing' not just the easiest thing. It holds up a mirror and reveals realities that need to be seen. To do this constructively, it teams with Navigator and together, they ensure a positive direction to their intervention. To do this with compassion, it teams with Empath and together they see the humanity in others. This combined constructive compassion builds relationships and is summed up perfectly in work 'I Thou' by the 20th century German philosopher and moralist Martin Buber. He looks at our attitude toward others. You either treat another as an 'It' (an object) or a 'Thou' (a whole person). As a 'Thou,' the other has their own needs, wants, and desires and you enter into a relationship of mutual respect. As an 'It,' my needs, wants and desires are more important, and others are merely a means to an end. As an 'It,' the other is seen as a collection of labels and qualities which are judged and used without regard for their humanity. This limits the potential of the self, others, and the relationship. The natural calling of constructive compassion of the mature Empath, Mentor and Navigator, is to treat the other as a whole person, a Thou. However, if not developed well, one betrays this calling and thinks or acts in self-interest. This betrayal is then supported by the voice of an undeveloped Inner Advisor, which speaks to defend the bad behaviour, thus encouraging a feedback loop of rationalising why such behaviour is acceptable. It is through the positive intent of Mentor, the positive interest in the success of others by Navigator, and the recognition of the humanity of others by the Empath that one moves from 'I It' to 'I Thou'.

In Shakespeare's play, 'The Tempest', the character Ariel (a spirit) acts as Mentor to his master Prospero, by encouraging him to act with mercy towards King Alonso. Prospero asks Ariel:

> *How fares the king and 's followers?*

to which Ariel guides:

> *Your charm so strongly works 'em that if you now beheld them, your affections would become tender.*

Prospero is guided, as he eventually proclaims:

> *The rarer action is in virtue than in vengeance. They being penitent, the sole drift of my purpose doth extend not a frown further. Go release them, Ariel. my charms I'll break, their senses I'll restore, and they shall be themselves.*

The children's novel and film Pinocchio shows a Mentor relationship between the puppet Pinocchio and Jiminy Cricket. To transform from a puppet to a real boy, Pinocchio must learn to think, feel and act truthfully. Becoming human requires courage to speak the truth and keep an Ethical position towards others. He is famously advised *to "Always let your conscience be your guide."* And it is Jiminy Cricket who is that conscience in the form of a Mentor.

See: Pinocchio and Jiminy Cricket – Always Let Your Conscience Be Your Guide in Good Leadership Book Movie Clips at:
https://www.youtube.com/c/goodleadership/playlists

Mentor and Leadership

In leadership, a Mentor grows the people around it with integrity. It does this by role-modelling values and acting fairly and justly. If called upon to explain a decision, it will be able to explain itself using a clearly defined set of principles. These principles, drawn from Inner Referee, are what it relies upon to Mentor others.

Often, in organisations, the way that people enter and leave is managed by an HR department. This makes them the typical organisational

Mentors. There are benefits to this, but it can also have a negative impact. Day-to-day leaders become distanced from the human relationship element of their organisation. They stop fulfilling the Mentor role. When this happens, it is easier for both leaders and followers to see each other as tools or objects. People become expendable. Employers use people solely to further their targets or profit margins. Employees see the employer as nothing but a wage giver. Malpractice and getting away with whatever you can becomes a norm, as long as it is hidden from HR. In this environment, moral behaviours descend, and people act badly towards one another without even noticing anything is wrong. Mentor is critical to the recruitment, selection, management, and development of people. Even in a disciplinary process, Mentor provides a route to a successful outcome. Mentor doesn't give up on others. It maintains the other's human rights to dignity and respect. Mentor is aware when their mentee is astray and will make a significant effort to bring them 'back to the fold.' Most people will accept they have done something wrong if treated fairly and with dignity. This builds psychological trust and openness around difficult issues. It makes the team more robust. Mentor is an ally in making sure that mistakes are not covered up and left to be discovered only when a crisis erupts.

Ethical dilemmas are part of our complex, multicultural world. We have already discussed the role of the Inner Referee in forming and holding our core values. As we engage in relationships, we realise that others have different core values. Mentor is key to being able to lead others in and through this complexity. People are troubled when they are required by their workplaces or relationships to breach deeply held values. Mentor understands this and finds ways to have an Ethical conversation that brings everyone to a more peaceful place. To do this well, Mentor needs to recognise values and ethics in terms of their universal validity.

Growing Up as Mentor

Your Mentor grows as you spend time learning about and then directing the moral growth of others. You are concerned about their 'doing good.' You build their character and conscience. You act as a mirror and take time out to influence others in this way. You become known as a principled guide. Over time, this becomes a natural part of your interaction with others.

The mature Mentor will have Depth in their Character. This is achieved through the 4Ls of development: Learn, Love, Lead and Live. Assess your Mentor by reflecting on the statements in the table.

Score yourself based on:		
1 = Never; 2 = Sometimes; 3 = Most of the time; 4 = Always		
LEARN	*I recognise and have a good understanding of the rights and values of other*	
LOVE	*I am passionate about the moral development of others*	
LEAD	*I am a guide for the moral well-being of others*	
LIVE	*I am respected and respectful*	

If you score 2 or below on any of the above, this is an area of development for you. Reflect using the guides below:

- **Learn: Recognise and have a good understanding of the rights and values of others.** Explore the world of those around you through the lens of values, rights, and principles. Take an interest in the moral standpoints of others and compare these against those you hold. Spend time outside of your moral comfort zone and listen to perspectives with which you do not agree. Reflect on these and how they influence behaviour. Be open to varied views whilst remaining anchored to what you know is right too.

- **Love: Be passionate about the moral development of others.** Be passionate about engaging with diverse people. Enjoy exploring moral challenges. Be open to growing and widening perspectives. Be comfortable around people with varied beliefs. Take pleasure in principled conversations and contentment in doing the right things for and with others.

- **Lead: Take an interest in and be a guide for the moral well-being of others.** Role model best behaviour. Give time to directing others towards what is right. Articulate, take on and manifest the principled position. Be aware of and compensate for unconscious and conscious bias. Give of your time freely in the pursuit of 'what is right.' Maintain a diversity of thought through maintaining diversity in your networks. Maintain a positive intention towards others; their growth, well-being, rights, respect and dignity.

- **Live: Be respected and respectful.** Be a natural moral compass for others. People gravitate towards you to 'keep themselves honest'. You are confident and comfortable articulating and living what you believe. You know where compromise is important and where it is dangerous. You are steadfast whilst maintaining flexibility. You are grounded whilst being open. You are non-judgmental whilst guiding towards better decisions. You recognise wrong from right whilst being open to changing your opinion. You are constantly learning more about yourself and your beliefs, alongside others and their beliefs.

A tool for exploring Mentor: I See You:

1. Think about someone who has had a profound positive influence on your life.

2. Reflect on 'what is the source of that influence?' 'How are/were they seeing you?'

3. You will find that for those who have had a significant impact on your life, it was usually 'how they saw you' as opposed to necessarily 'what they said.' They see you as a whole 'person' (a Thou) and not an object, statistic, or label (an It).

4. Now let's apply this way of 'being' with others around you.

5. Identify someone around you who you feel is being an obstacle or difficult for you.

6. Change the way you are 'seeing' this person. See the whole person and not just the action or position. Think about the person you identified in number 1 above and how they see/saw you. Project this way of being in the way you are seeing the new person.

7. Now reconsider the situation you are in afresh. What new options have emerged? How can you change how you are seeing, behaving and being in the situation? What can you do proactively to Mentor in this situation?

More tools available in The Good Leadership Development Programme at www.goodleadership.org.

Relationship with the Inner Domain (Inner Referee)

There is a unique relationship that exists between the Inner Referee and the Mentor. This level of interdependence is exclusive to the Dimension of Ethics. A developed Inner Referee not only enables Mentor, but also legitimises it too. It forms the repository from which to draw reference for interactions with others. But also acts as a reference point for others to validate your credentials as Mentor. In guiding others, you are checking yourself too. If your Mentor is not aligned with your Inner Referee, your heart, body, mind and spirit will be letting you know. You will feel uncomfortable, and this would be sensed by those around you too.

Summary

Mentor is an enabler of others by championing equality and diversity in human endeavours. Mentor proactively supports others to become the best they can be and helps them back onto the right moral pathway when they veer away. Mentor says, 'do what is right, not what is easy' and supports others in doing the right thing by making the journey with them. Mentor connects fundamental human rights on a personal level, not only a legal one, and influences others to do the same. Mentor's key role is to lead the way on how to increase Ethical behaviour. Mentor collaborates with the other three 'Domain of Others' Characters in the following ways:

- Mentor gives Storyteller the opportunity to positively influence another. It then provides further stories that can be used by Storyteller to impact on others.
- Mentor gives Empath the opportunity to explore the diversity of values and principles held by different people. This gives Empath deeper insights into others.
- Mentor gives Navigator a measure of the correctness of the direction of others.

NAVIGATOR

Navigator resides in the Domain of Others and the Dimension of Purpose.

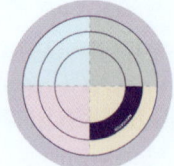

Who?

It takes a genuine interest in other peoples' goals and visions, supporting them to hold on to and achieve them. Navigator helps people find direction when the going gets tough. It travels alongside them as a trusted companion providing the encouragement and strength needed to reach their destination. Purpose and vision come best to us in metaphor and images - the language of poets and mystics. Thus, Navigator shows up in unexpected places, we just need to be open to its messages and meanings. It doesn't have to be human and can be signs and symbols from nature too. In Viktor Frankl's deeply resonant book, 'Man's Search for Meaning,' he recounts the way that a small bird acted as a Navigator. It gave him hope through the dark days of incarceration in one of the Nazi death camps during the Second World War. For Frankl, the bird was a way to communicate with his wife who had been killed in a women's camp nearby. The bird accompanied Frankl during the days of hard labour. It provided a lifeline and connection to something outside of the hell hole. It acted as a reminder that there is hope for the future and a reason to survive. Navigator's leadership role is to guide others to help achieve their Purpose.

Say and Do?

Motto: *'I Will help you achieve'*

Navigator has an interest in helping others arrive at their rightful destination. Navigators are often professional coaches, versed in a range of skills that help individuals and organisations find their True North. Navigators can also be a friend, family member or even someone who comes into your life for a limited time and makes a profound impact. The common quality is that Navigator shines a light on your passions and reminds you where you need to be heading. Navigator sustains hopefulness and a focus on the light at the end of the tunnel and walks the path with you. As such, Navigator is interested in seeing you succeed; opening doors, making connections, and steering situations to make this happen. Navigator asks, 'What are you trying to achieve?', 'Why is this so important to you?', 'How will that make you feel?', 'Who else can help you get there?' All are questions to help get clarity for Purpose.

Portrait

The Purpose dimension in leadership connects people to firm targets. It clarifies the mission and drives towards resolute goals. Navigator recognises this across Domains. It identifies another's personal Purpose and helps align this to a systemic or organisational Purpose. When organisations have a strong Navigator, there is a flow of energy through the whole. Navigator creates dynamism and a shared will. It harnesses aspiration and uses it to drive towards a common Purpose to succeed. Volunteers, employees, stakeholders, and partners align. Working alongside Mentor, Navigator develops people who commit and go the extra mile. If Navigator helps set the direction, Mentor assesses the correctness of that direction. If Navigator drives things forward, Mentor ensures people feel appreciated and respected.

In Shakespeare's play Macbeth, we see Lady Macbeth as Navigator steering Macbeth through his doubts and worries about his pathway to the crown. In a private moment, she reflects on her husband's nature:

> *Glamis thou art, and Cawdor; and shalt be what thou are promised. Yet do I fear thy nature: it is too full o'th milk of human kindness to catch the nearest way: thou wouldst be great, art not without ambition, but without the illness should attend it.*

Lady Macbeth as Navigator to her husband, is formidable. She finds whatever route she can to hold him to his (and her) Inner Visionary dream. The dilemma of the play and its central drama is the tussle between Purpose and Ethics; Macbeth's Inner Referee versus Lady Macbeth's Navigator.

A film to increase awareness of the positive enabling that is central to Navigator is Mary Poppins. Mary, an archetypal Navigator, comes to the Banks family home to care for the children. In her role as their Nanny, she rekindles their sense of hope in life and helps them believe that anything is possible.

> See: Mary Poppins in Good Leadership Book Movie Clips at:
> https://www.youtube.com/c/goodleadership/playlists

Navigator and Leadership

Leaders must enable and help their followers to fulfil their potential. They need to be the Navigator of other peoples' vision and Purpose. Money, power, and position are frequently thought of as the main drivers for success in the workplace - this is not the full picture. They are incidental to the actual Purpose. In fact, if this belief is encouraged, people remain unfulfilled. Navigator challenges norms in such environments. The leader as Navigator will help you find your passion. They will encourage and facilitate the uncovering of your true calling. This may indeed lead to money, power, and position too, but supplementary to the achievement of a higher goal. A leader as Navigator will help people clarify a vision with added value, erring on the side of greatness. They will then find a commonality between this and the corporate Purpose. They craft an inclusive partnership between an organisation and its people. They make people feel like they are in control of their journey and that the organisation is conspiring to help them grow. When this is missing, talented people leave organisations. They look for opportunities where their passion and Purpose are encouraged, not suppressed.

Growing Up as Navigator

Your Navigator grows as you spend time assisting others. You are concerned about the success of others. You help people achieve and open networks for them. You guide and coach to build capacity and ease attainment. You become known as a helper and facilitator. Over time, you naturally help advance others in their life journeys.

The mature Navigator will have Depth in their Character. This is achieved through the 4Ls of development: Learn, Love, Lead and Live. Assess your Navigator through reflecting on the statements in the table.

Score yourself based on:		
1 = Never; 2 = Sometimes; 3 = Most of the time; 4 = Always		
LEARN	*I see value in the vision of others*	
LOVE	*I take a genuine interest in the vision of others*	
LEAD	*I am a guide, facilitator and capacity builder for others to achieve their fullest potential*	
LIVE	*I am a consummate helper and door-opener*	

If you score 2 or below on any of the above, this is an area of development for you. Reflect using the guides below:

- Learn: **See the value of the vision of others.** Value how they dovetail with your own and wider visions. Understand that the success of the whole brings with it the success of individuals and vice versa. Explore how you can facilitate others to achieve their missions.

- Love: **Take an interest in the vision of others.** Be interested when things go well. Take time to enquire into what made that goal or milestone achievable. Is that an experience that can be transferred to other areas of life as well? Take joy in these enquiries. Be optimistic for others. Be satisfied when you have assisted another in this way. Enjoy the reciprocity that emerges when you Navigate for others.

- Lead: **Guide, facilitate and capacity build others to achieve their fullest potential.** Encourage others in their pursuits, providing them with contacts and opportunities. Remove barriers. When another is finding the going tough, support them. Remind them of where they are heading, cheer them on and believe in their ability to reach their goals. Coach them, and if things don't work out, help them see what has gone well and what could be done differently next time.

- Live: **Be a consummate helper and door opener.** Become the natural go to person for support. People come to you because they know they will be assisted. You motivate and inspire. You know what needs to be done and drive towards it, bringing others with you.

A tool for exploring Navigator: Visualisation:

1. This is an exercise best done as a coach to assist another to visualise their future. Give the following instructions / ask the questions:
2. Close your eyes and imagine you wake up 20 years from now in your preferred future.
3. Where did you wake up?
4. Who else was there?
5. What can you see? Describe your surroundings.
6. How do you travel around?
7. You go for a walk…. where are you going and where do you pass? Who do you meet and what do you do?
8. What are you proud of having achieved?
9. What is your work environment like? Your personal environment? Your community environment?

This exercise can be combined with the Inner Visionary exercise to 'draw your vision' for further clarity too.

More tools are available in The Good Leadership Development Programme at www.goodleadership.org.

Relationship with the Inner Domain (Inner Visionary)

There is an exchange between Inner Visionary and Navigator in that they often enable one another. Navigator would have, within its portfolio of personal Purpose, the passion for helping others realise their potential. As such, Navigator is fulfilling the need of the Inner Visionary, and the Inner Visionary is driving the activities of Navigator. This relationship is not as intertwined as we found in the Mentor / Inner Referee dynamic, as there may be other drivers at work. The passion for helping others may be an offshoot of a related Purpose. For example, to help minority groups achieve in a field where they are under-represented. As such, Inner Visionary is driving Navigator, not because of a general passion, but a more defined one.

Summary

Navigator is the trusted companion that helps others stay true to living a purposeful life. It will help you find, clarify, articulate, and achieve your vision. Navigator opens doors and motivates others to keep going when things get difficult. Navigator is genuinely interested in what gives energy and vitality to a person. It helps you achieve dreams by breaking them into goals and attaining them. The key role of Navigator is to champion purposeful action, provide encouragement and give confidence to others. Navigator collaborates with the other three 'Domain of Others' Characters in the following ways:

- Navigator gives Storyteller the opportunity to motivate and inspire another.
- Navigator allows Empath to gain insights into another's passions and motivation.
- Navigator gives Mentor information about another's direction of travel. It allows Mentor to identify challenges and mitigate against potential moral consequences that may arise.

STORYTELLER

Storyteller resides in the Domain of Others and the Dimension of Communication.

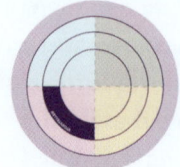

Who?

Its talent is to structure narratives that make connections, attract, and influence people. Storyteller can make mundane information interesting, engaging, and relevant. It knows how to shape Communication so that it lands on receptive ears. Storyteller collects appealing stories, providing powerful content for the range of Communication platforms available.

It constructs messages by paying attention to narrative, tone, body language and style. Storyteller is an influencer par excellence. People respond to stories; we allow them to enter our imaginations and hearts in ways that factual information does not. Storyteller knows this. It presents information in a way certain to move the recipient. This power to influence is more potent when coupled with the Understanding of the Empath. Together, Storyteller and Empath would know the right buttons, nuances, and references to impact the listener. Its leadership role is to find the right language with which you identify. Whether that be to hold up a mirror for you to recognise and reflect or shine a light to inspire and motivate.

Say and Do?

Motto: *'I will help you understand'*

Storyteller provides the voice for what needs to be heard and finds a range of ways that the messages can be received. Storyteller's power lies in matching the means of Communication to the message. It can turn words into tools to persuade and motivate others. It makes a message convincing and credible. It can influence mood through powerful narratives, bringing hope to difficult situations, comfort to those in despair, or urgency when action is needed. It allows leaders to rally the troops behind a mission, salespeople to compel customers in to closing a deal, and marketeers to encourage a call to action.

Storyteller can aid understanding and insight when appealing to the mind, trigger emotion when appealing to the heart, and inspire the imagination in appealing to the spirit. A developed Storyteller is versatile. It sells. It persuades. It inspires. It explains. It comforts. It knows when to speak and when to listen. It takes content from others and gives it an impactful language.

Storyteller is the Character that lets the world know what you are thinking, feeling, and intending. It requires diction, expression, pitch, tone, and body language. Storyteller enjoys verbal swordplay, the argument in and of itself.

Working with the Empath, Storyteller understands its audience. It chooses appropriate language, symbols, metaphors, and styles that will best land a message. With Mentor, Storyteller will speak truth to power and voice what is right and fair. In collaboration with Navigator, Storyteller can inspire others to keep going, act with courage and bring people together for a common cause.

Portrait

Studying the way actors approach a character can give a good insight into Storyteller. Notice the way they use body language and voice to communicate both the inner life and outer behaviours of those they are portraying. They bring their whole person to invoke the right response in you. There needs to be congruence for the audience to accept the character as credible. The same applies to Storyteller and a leader.

Communication has become a competitive sport in our world. There are so many voices and images clamouring to be noticed. Finding a way to tailor your messages so that they cut through the surrounding noise is a challenge. The ability for a message to land is a combination of finding the right language, for the right audience, at the right time, and presenting it in the right way. Storyteller thinks about the who, what, where, when and why of the Communication. It gives both the transmitter and receiver equal importance.

In Shakespeare's Julius Caesar, Storyteller is used to influence the people of Rome. Following Caesar's murder, Brutus uses it to calm and convince them that the murder was justified. However, Mark Anthony follows, showing an even greater competency as Storyteller and stirs the crowd to eventually force the conspirators to flee the city. Brutus speaks in prose, the language of the lower ranks:

> *Romans, countrymen, and lovers! Hear me for my cause, and be silent that you may hear. Believe me for mine honor, and have respect to mine honor that you may believe. Censure me in your wisdom, and awake your senses that you may the better judge. If there be any in this assembly, any dear friend of Caesar's, to him I say that Brutus' love to Caesar was no less than his. If then that friend demand why Brutus rose against Caesar, this is my answer: not that I loved Caesar less, but that I loved Rome more.*

Mark Anthony speaks in verse, using repetition, rhythm and emphasis:

> *Friends, Romans, countrymen, lend me your ears. I come to bury Caesar, not to praise him. The evil that men do lives after them; the good is oft interred with their bones. So let it be with Caesar. The noble Brutus hath told you Caesar was ambitious. If it were so, it was a grievous fault, and grievously hath Caesar answered it. Here, under leave of Brutus and the rest for Brutus is an honorable man; so are they all, all honorable men come I to speak in Caesar's funeral. He was my friend, faithful and just to me. But Brutus says he was ambitious, and Brutus is an honorable man.*
> *He hath brought many captives home to Rome whose ransoms did the general coffers fill. Did this in Caesar seem ambitious? When that the poor have cried, Caesar hath wept. Ambition should be made of sterner stuff.*

Brutus talks about himself, whereas Mark Anthony elevates the funeral speech to invoke values that are important to the people themselves. He includes Brutus in the speech and in doing so, turns the argument against him. This is Storyteller at its most compelling.

In the film Dead Poets Society, John Keating, the character played by Robin Williams, sells the boys something they didn't think they needed nor wanted. A new way of using and appreciating language! He uses the persuasive power of Storyteller and inspires his students to appreciate historic Storytellers too. Through articulation, emphasis, passion, posture, innovation, tone, and resonance with the receiver, he wins hearts and minds with a narrative that penetrates deep into their spirit.

> See: Dead Poets Society in Good Leadership Book Movie Clips at:
> https://www.youtube.com/c/goodleadership/playlists

Storyteller and Leadership

Leadership involves influencing one another to move towards a certain future. As such, the leader, as Storyteller, builds trust, rapport, and motivation to be part of a bigger story. Using language that explains and aligns with organisational Understanding, Purpose, and Ethics. To inspire both when opportunities are abundant and when times are difficult. Storyteller is the leader's mouthpiece. It articulates the mind of the Characters of the other Dimensions. It presents its messages using the appropriate vocal delivery, body language, energy, emotional connectivity, and creativity.

Influenced by a developed Inner Referee, Mentor, and Custodian - the Characters of the Ethics Dimension - it champions integrity and presents as an authentic leader. It allows the public consolidation and validation of principles and values. It advocates justice and fairness. It speaks truth to power and adds humility to key messages.

Influenced by a developed Inner Visionary, Navigator, and Architect - the Characters of the Purpose Dimension - it arouses others and presents as an inspirational leader. It motivates towards a positive goal. It sells the vision. It drives Purpose and ensures followers remain steadfast on the road to achievement.

Influenced by a developed Inner Master, Empath, and Oracle - the Characters of the Understanding Dimension - it acts as a guide and presents as an insightful leader. It educates. It presents the complex in an easy-to-understand way. It gives both content and process. It provides instructions to navigate even the most difficult challenges. It exposes mistakes and turning points but then explains consequences and communicates learning. In doing so, it gives insights critical for informed decisions and commitment.

Growing Up as Storyteller

Your Storyteller influences people. You articulate your Understanding, your Ethics, and your Purpose. It is your voice in the outside world. You use it to arouse and to calm; to persuade and concede. To reinforce what you stand for and guide you on what must change. It speaks about who you are whilst focusing on who you are speaking to. As you become more fluent you become a 'live' Storyteller.

The mature Storyteller will have Depth in their Character. This is achieved through the 4Ls of development: Learn, Love, Lead and Live.

Assess your Storyteller by reflecting on the statements in the table.

Score yourself based on:		
1 = Never; 2 = Sometimes; 3 = Most of the time; 4 = Always		
LEARN	I am aware of the impact of narratives on others	
LOVE	I have a joy in interacting with others	
LEAD	I am articulate and relatable	
LIVE	I am turned-in to others	

If you score 2 or below on any of the above, this is an area of development for you. Reflect using the guides below:

- **Learn: Aware of the impact narratives have on others.** Develop the style, humour, emphasis, and cultural references that make your message personal. Develop an extensive vocabulary and understand the different modes to convey your message.

- **Love: Take pleasure in interacting with others.** You enjoy giving stimulus and the response it gives. You develop a taste for experimenting with different tones, dialects, and languages.

- **Lead: Articulate and relatable.** You deploy a range of storytelling patterns to get impact. You resonate with your audience. You build rapport by pacing your message and effectively influence through moderating your delivery.

- **Live: Tuned in to others.** You are naturally flexible in style, tone, pitch, and vocabulary achieving the desired impact. You are comfortable in and leverage the culture around you. People gravitate to you and are at ease with you because of what you have to say and how you say it.

A tool for exploring Storyteller: Presenting well:

Here are some top tips for speaking in public well:

1. **Use your body:** be open and relaxed. Move smoothly with body posture and head erect but not stiff. Hold genuine eye contact.

2. **Use your time:** make the first 30 seconds count. Take time…land before you launch. Don't forget to breathe. Hold short pauses before speaking, then speak in complete sentences.

3. **Use your energy:** engage your passion and vision and unlock its power.

4. **Use your voice:** vary your pace and slow down so that people can take in what you are saying. Pause after an important point to let it sink in further. Let your voice change pitch to distinguish the different things you are saying. Use inflexion to ask questions, not to make statements. Emphasise the keyword in a sentence to give clarity to your content.

5. **Use your words:**

Sparking action: Using the language of the Navigator, describe how a successful change was implemented in the past and allow listeners to imagine how it might work in their situation. Place the listener in an imaginative 'What if?' and 'This could be our story too' scenario.

Communicating who you are: Using the language of the Empath, provide the audience with engaging drama. Reveal some strength or vulnerability. This will help to transform perceptions and build trust.

Transmitting values: Using the language of the Mentor, build a familiarity and rapport with the audience. Prompt discussion about the issues raised by the value being promoted. It galvanizes the rightness of actions: 'That's so right!' 'Why don't we do that all the time?'

Fostering collaboration: Using the language of the Conductor, recount a situation that listeners have also experienced. This prompts them to share their own stories about the topic. The swapping of stories creates a narrative chain reaction that is a powerful call to action. Use multiple platforms and routes for contribution.

Taming the grapevine: Using the language of the Custodian, highlight some aspect of a rumour that reveals it to be untrue or unreasonable.

Sharing knowledge: Using the language of the Oracle, focus on problems and show, in some detail, how they are corrected. Solicit alternative and possibly better solutions. 'Gosh! We'd better watch out for that in the future.

Leading people into the future: Using the language of the Architect, evoke the future you want to create. Paint a positive and inspiring vision of the future.

More tools are available in The Good Leadership Development Programme at www.goodleadership.org.

Relationship with the Inner Domain (Inner Advisor)

Storyteller controls our articulation. It can drown out all other voices, including that of Inner Advisor. The quality and level of development of both will dictate how and what each presents to others. Storyteller relies upon Inner Advisor as the voice that explains what is happening both inwardly and outwardly. A developed Inner Advisor will ensure it is heard, drawing on the other Characters from other Dimensions. The responsibility for Inner Advisor to be heard, however, is with both Storyteller and Inner Advisor itself. An impatient Storyteller may speak first and think later. An alignment of messages will ensure fluency - the voice inside your head needs to support the voice coming out of it.

Summary

Storyteller experiences joy in engagement with others and sharing meaningful and purposeful narratives. It considers and selects its words with care. It tries to influence by employing a full range of skills and techniques. It owns its stories, understands their relevance, and knows how to Communicate them to others. The key role of Storyteller is to command the tools of personal Communication to accurately portray the leadership message. Storyteller collaborates with the other three 'Domain of Others' Characters in the following ways:

- Storyteller gives Empath a stimulating tool which allows a deeper Understanding of others.
- Storyteller gives Mentor the language to guide and present the correctness of situations to others.
- Storyteller gives Navigator the capacity and competency to articulate in a way that motivates others.

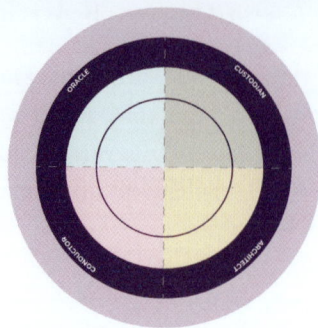

Characters in the Domain of Context

ORACLE

Oracle resides in the Domain of Context and the Dimension of Understanding.

Who?

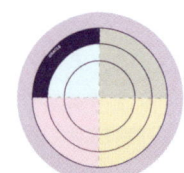

It Understands the world as it is and perceives reality clearly. It accurately reads complex systems that influence the way individuals, teams, and organisations behave. It grasps how layers relate to each other and how parts connect to the whole. Oracle can appear to predict the future but is simply a few steps ahead of those with less Understanding.

Oracle's talent is for raising awareness of what is present in system dynamics. Every person belongs to a web of interrelating systems: family, work, organisations, communities, countries, political systems, ecosystem and even the solar system. This matrix of systems is intricate. Oracle's leadership role is to bring an Understanding of how these all have a bearing on each other.

Say and Do?

Motto: *'That Makes Sense'*

Oracle is the sense-maker of an organisation. It notices what systems dominate in any given situation. For example, if an organisation is seeking to change its product development, there needs to be awareness of who the customers are; what are their current needs; what might be influencing those needs; whether that will change in the foreseeable future; who competitors might be; whether the organisation has the capacity to make the changes. Multiple forces influence decisions, and Oracle approaches each from the widest possible perspective and deepest Understanding. This awareness makes it easier to know where to direct energy in a productive way. Oracle is the Character that has contact with all the subsystems within the system, and can align the smaller units with the larger ones. It thus increases opportunities for organisations to work in flow with their settings. When systems are aligned an energetic flow moves through the whole. It feels like swimming with the tide, not against it. Oracle would say: 'I understand how this all fits together' and 'I know how to get this moving'.

Portrait

Oracle is very comfortable with context. It engages well with shifting landscapes. It enables leaders to make sense of available choices within the matrix of contending forces. Oracle networks with a wide range of stakeholders. It looks for solutions that keep whole systems in a healthy state of balance. It connects the dots in a structured and ordered way. It is crucial to providing clarity in a world of growing complexity.

Oracle enables a wide-angled view of any given situation and Understands that a problem can also contain a solution. For example, suppose a client raises a complaint about a service received from your organisation. Oracle will take a step back from the initial impulse to respond to the complaint head on. It would explore if this issue is related to other, more hidden, dynamics. Let's imagine the client had thought that the service would open new income streams and that is slow to happen, putting pressure on his business. He needs to find a way to unlock his system and is blaming your service. Or this client feels responsible for supporting his team and has not noticed that they have not implemented the correct processes that your product requires. Or maybe there is a flaw in your own system, but it is not at the service level but in a supply chain. Oracle will seek to find a solution that enables the relationship with the client to settle in its right place; to avoid humiliation of individuals or teams, and to identify holistic issues and solutions.

In Shakespeare's play, you see Hamlet's Oracle in his Understanding of a new Denmark. His father is part of the old order of warrior leaders where the laws of family honour and revenge dominate. Hamlet belongs to a more thoughtful and questioning worldview. He seeks out truths to make peace with his enemies. He is open and aware of emerging and trending issues and the need for a newer type of leadership. Tragically, he and his opponent in a dual Laertes, both die at the end of the play, but not before doing what it takes to make peace with each other and to stop the rot that was destroying Denmark. Had he lived; he would have 'proved most royal.'

Laertes: Exchange forgiveness with me, noble Hamlet. mine and my father's death come not upon thee, nor thine on me!
Hamlet: Heaven make thee free of it! I follow thee.

In more contemporary stories, you can see Oracle in action, in the film 'The Matrix.' The enlightened Neo sees individual parts, their connections and how the whole performs in the system of The Matrix. He makes sense of the world around him through Understanding and insight.

See: The Matrix in Good Leadership Book Movie Clips at:
https://www.youtube.com/c/goodleadership/playlists

In the film Limitless, the central character Eddie Morra, played by Bradley Cooper, can enhance perception and Understanding (albeit through illicit means). He makes sense of the world around him through the Character qualities of the Oracle. He famously states, *"I see 50 scenarios which puts me 50 steps ahead of you"*. Oracle can assess stakeholders, connections, probabilities, and risk in order to 'scenario plan' and consider the consequences - an important leadership function.

See: Limitless in Good Leadership Book Movie Clips at:
https://www.youtube.com/c/goodleadership/playlists

Oracle and Leadership

Leaders must be attuned to the apparent and hidden forces in an organisation. All systems are a collection of parts and relationships making up a whole. The nature of these parts and relationships dictates what emerges from that system. Leaders thus need to Understand them. Once this is done, the effect of any intervention into the system can be foreseen. Without such an Understanding, the leader remains at the mercy of an architecture that may seem to behave unpredictably. This applies to the people, processes and even the physical assets of any organisation. How is each identified or categorised? How do they relate to each other and to the wider context? What or who influences what or whom? Consider history, connectivity, communication, geography, and time.

Whole system thinking is important to address emerging issues in the workplace. For example, increased use of automation, in particular Artificial Intelligence (AI), is having a significant impact on unemployment and redeployment of the workforce. Looking at such phenomena systemically will ensure holistic solutions and mitigate potential negative fallout. Leaders lead change. Oracle enables leaders to lead change in a systemic way.

Growing Up as Oracle

As you become more aware of your surroundings, your Oracle grows. You start to see how the whole relates to the parts. You become increasingly comfortable with complexity and multiple settings. You leverage the appropriate networks for effective problem solving. You become familiar with your context and how it works.

The mature Oracle will have Depth in their Character. This is achieved through the 4Ls of development: Learn, Love, Lead and Live. Assess your Oracle through reflecting on the statements in the table.

Score yourself based on:		
1 = Never; 2 = Sometimes; 3 = Most of the time; 4 = Always		
LEARN	I Understand contextual frames of reference and how things work and what needs to be done	
LOVE	I am passionate in engaging with the outside world	
LEAD	I engage, network, connect and leverage people, organisations, and systems	
LIVE	I am competent, confident and comfortable in my surroundings	

If you score 2 or below on any of the above, this is an area of development for you. Reflect using the guides below:

- **Learn: Have a good Understanding of the contextual frames of reference.** You Understand how things work and what needs to be done. Zoom out and take a bird's eye view of your situation: What are the systemic challenges and solutions? What are the wider patterns that influence and impinge upon individuals and teams? What are the relationships between the individual parts? How does energy flow through the linkages? What are the hidden dynamics of organisations and networks?

- **Love: Be passionate about engaging your world.** Take time to explore parts, connections, networks and the whole. Be confident that the system will always behave properly, according to its components. Experiment and marvel at the beauty of complexity.

- **Lead: Engage, network, connect and leverage people, organisations, and systems.** Adopt and adapt to new information as it emerges. Understand the rules that govern your system to influence it through strategic interventions.

- **Live: Be competent in your surroundings.** Be confident in your ability to operate well in your system. Be comfortable with complexity. Accept the realities and emergence. Be a lifelong learner, seeker, and influencer of your system.

A tool for exploring Oracle: Systems mapping:

Whole System Thinking is a tool for Understanding how different parts relate to one another. How they influence each other in the 'whole system.' Think about the climate, for example. How the sun, air, water, soil, plants, animals, and people affect it and thus impact each other. They all belong to a 'whole system,' and it is important to Understand how they relate, positively and negatively, to each other. The following exercise helps you explore a systemic map for a challenge or issue:

1. You will need a pad of sticky notes, a sheet of flip chart paper and a pen.

2. Think about the question or system you would like to investigate, write it on a sticky note and place it in the centre of the paper.

3. Write all the elements affecting the challenge on individual notes (include yourself) and lay them around the challenge.
4. Consider each and group some together based on commonalities or linkages. Use your intuition if you do not see any apparent linkages.
5. Bring notes closer together or farther apart depending upon their relatedness. Take notice of the spacing between elements. You may even change the direction they are facing if appropriate.
6. Draw linkages between the central note and between the individual elemental notes too.
7. Look at your map from a bird's eye perspective. Consider the influence of each element and its relationship to others. Consider the linkages that are twice or thrice removed too. What indirect actions does one element have on another or on the central issue?
8. Walk around it and view it from different angles. What else captures your interest and attention? What do you notice about the flow of energy through your map?

Consider moving some of the elements to bring them to an arrangement that feels more satisfying and balanced. What does this reveal to you about your challenge and potential solution?

Systemic thinking can show indirect routes to problem-solving and reveals where the system is blocked.

More tools are available in The Good Leadership Development Programme at www.goodleadership.org.

Relationship with Domain of Others (Empath)

In the Dimension of Understanding, we have already explored the relationship between Inner Master and Empath. What, then, is the relationship between Oracle and Empath, which connects all three? As you move outward, each Domain increases in complexity. If the relationship as Empath is bilateral, for Oracle it is multilateral. Oracle needs to Understand the connections between others in the system as much as the individuals themselves. It relies on Empath to give it these insights but needs to look wider and deeper at infrastructure and environment too. Both Empath and Oracle assist one another in this deeper Understanding. Empath gives Oracle information about how others feel and interact with the system. Oracle gives Empath insight into the context that is influencing people. This flow of information is essential to get the level of insight necessary for leadership.

Summary

Oracle connects the dots in systems. It Understands that the whole behaves differently and is more than the sum of its parts. It Understands that the relationship between these parts accounts for this difference. It notices and participates enthusiastically in networks that hold organisations and systems together. In a complex world, it provides insights and connections. Its key role is to know how various parts of a whole fit and work together. Oracle collaborates with the other three 'Domain of Context' Characters in the following ways:

- Oracle gives Conductor the Understanding it needs to ensure a fuller and wider dissemination of its message.
- Oracle gives Custodian the insight into the wider system and thus, how to positively impact it for good.
- Oracle gives Architect insights into how a system works for it to move it in the direction the Architect desires.

CUSTODIAN

Custodian resides in the Domain of Context and the Dimension of Ethics.

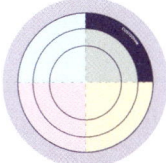

Who?

It is the champion of equality and fairness. Custodian ensures that individuals and teams adhere to key moral principles that sit at the heart of families, organisations, and communities. It is the guardian of what truly matters. It cares passionately for the integrity of the whole unit. It ensures that decency and respect are part of a system's development. It is responsible for a conscience that is fair to all stakeholders.

Custodian's leadership role is to safeguard the 'rightness of the direction' an organisation and society are moving towards. It will raise awareness of when values and standards are not followed.

Say and Do?

Motto: *'Let's Leave a Positive Legacy'*

Custodian holds the beating heart of an organisation. It keeps the flow of energy going in a positive direction. Custodian is a lover of truth. It takes pleasure in being in the presence of those who seek to put down their biases and prejudices for a more joyful and inclusive society. The Dalai Lama comes to mind as an example of a great Custodian. He is most frequently seen going about his business with great joy and tranquillity despite being banished from his homeland.

Portrait

Custodian protects the universal rights of all, especially the most vulnerable. It is true to the spirit of the law and would even challenge legal frameworks if they took people away from truths or did not have universal application.

Custodian is the guardian of core principles yet would also be aware of those which can flex. This ensures inclusivity whilst holding fast to defining values. It promotes diversity within systems and allows organisations to be adaptive; finding a balance between their founding Purpose and the changing needs of contemporary society. Successful religious or educational institutions and systems of government are all relevant case studies to see Custodians in action. It has a crucial role in challenging systemic inequalities. By increasing respect for people, Custodian ensures diversity is a heart-based value, not just a legal requirement. It builds an environment of care and compassion. It has a passion for a better world for all. Custodian is a peace maker and the guardian of what is right.

In Shakespeare's 'Measure for Measure', the play examines the relationship between morality and mercy in the city of Vienna. Despite having laws to guide the people, Duke Vincentio has allowed them to go unenforced and the city is in chaos:

> *We have strict statutes and most biting laws. The needful bits and curbs to headstrong weeds, which for this nineteen years we have let slip; even like an o'ergrown lion in a cave, that goes not out to prey. Now, as fond fathers, having bound up the threatening twigs of birch, only to stick it in their children's sight for terror, not to use, in time the rod becomes more mock'd than fear'd; so our decrees, dead to infliction, to themselves are dead; and liberty plucks justice by the nose; the baby beats the nurse, and quite athwart Goes all decorum.*

The Duke departs leaving Angelo to rule the city who begins enforcing strict laws to curb the immorality. He goes too far, and the Duke disguises himself as a friar to discover how society is reacting to Angelo's strict ruling. The title of the play, 'Measure for Measure' applies to the moral mercy that the Duke instils when he returns to power. As Custodian, he finds a balance between competing societal values to bring stability to Vienna.

A contemporary film to watch to see Custodian in action is 'Selma'. It tells the story of Martin Luther King Jr. and the civil rights movement in the USA. A Custodian speaks truth to power for the benefit of a wider cause (organisation, society, or world). He leads from a position that 'enough is enough.' A Custodian is the caretaker for what is right and serves a larger Ethical position. MLK inspires a movement and unites diverse supporters. He catalyses a change in the whole of society and provides a compass for future generations. He, despite challenge and threat, stays true to a core value of non-violence but flexes where appropriate to agitate the unjust law.

> See: Selma In Good Leadership Book Movie Clips at:
> https://www.youtube.com/c/goodleadership/playlists

Custodian and Leadership

Canon Dr Edmund Newall gave a sermon on the subject of 'Disagreeing Well' and the challenge that the Custodians of the Church of England face when it comes to contentious issues.

"We are told by Jesus in the Sermon on the Mount that, in his Kingdom, peacemakers will be blessed. When we disagree with each other it's easy for us to use words like bullets. But, if we take seriously our role as peacemakers, our words can build bridges over which we can meet each other and learn to disagree in a different way, to disagree well."

To retain influence, our institutions need to respond intelligently, and with appropriate prudence, to constantly changing social and political demographics. Custodian, working with Oracle, brings this Understanding, ensuring inclusivity and thereby lays the foundations both for peace and human development. Secular institutions, such as the United Nations, are tasked with similar responsibilities, as expressed by their former Secretary General, Kofi Annan:

"We may have different religions, different coloured skin, but we all belong to one human race" and *"We have the means and the capacity to deal with our problems, if only we can find the political will."*

Custodian is the territory of the peacemaker who is unafraid of what others might think. They take seriously their role in safeguarding the needs of the next generation. They are optimistic about the goodness of people to do the right thing. Highlighted well in the words of Yusuf Cat Stevens:

"Oh, I've been smiling lately dreaming about the world as one, and I believe it could be, someday it's going to come."
Peace Train

Growing your Custodian

You are a servant to those around you. An organisational citizen. You are concerned with fairness and justice in society. You bring people together, build relationships and harmony. You take responsibility for the sustainable growth of yourself, your people, and your community. You consider correct intentions, means and consequences.

The mature Custodian will have Depth in their Character. This is achieved through the 4Ls of development: Learn, Love, Lead and Live. Assess your Custodian by reflecting on the statements in the table.

Score yourself based on:		
1 = Never; 2 = Sometimes; 3 = Most of the time; 4 = Always		
LEARN	*I understand the principles and laws in society*	
LOVE	*I take responsibility for the world around me*	
LEAD	*I serve others and uphold universal Ethical principles*	
LIVE	*I have a sustained commitment to the success of communities and the well-being of the planet*	

If you score 2 or below on any of the above, this is an area of development for you. Reflect using the guides below:

- **Learn: You develop a good understanding of the laws that govern society.** A solid grasp of universal principles and their application. You understand the long-term and short-term moral impact of actions. You consider the consequences on minorities. You research sustainable solutions to problems.

- **Love: You are nurturing and willingly take responsibility for the world.** You are passionate about the growth of people and society. You recognise and appreciate positive moral action around you. You are comfortable discussing the 'undiscussable'. You are encouraged by opportunities to spread 'goodness.' You flourish when pushed to explore new moral thresholds and encourage the exploration in those around you too.

- **Lead: You serve others and uphold universal Ethical principles.** You champion diversity and inclusion. You delegate responsibilities and then step back. You plan your succession so that power is distributed, and responsibilities are shared. You establish moral standards in your organisation and processes to raise the capabilities of people to reach them. You encourage challenge and protect whistle blowers. You invest in the well-being of the people in your organisation.

- **Live: You have a commitment to the success of communities and the planet.** Environmentalism, sustainability, and the growth of individuals form part of your strategies. You are the organisation's moral compass.

A tool for exploring Custodian: The Trolley Ethical Problem:

There are many Ethical puzzles that can be explored to 'flex your Custodian muscles.' The Trolley Problem is one which has been used to highlight different philosophical thoughts:

There is a runaway trolley on a railway track. Ahead of it are five people tied to the track and unable to move. If the trolley reaches them, they will die. You are standing next to a lever. If you pull this lever, the trolley will switch to a different set of tracks. You notice that there is one person on this new side track. You have two options:

1. Do nothing and allow the trolley to kill the five people on the main track.

2. Pull the lever, diverting the trolley onto the side track, where it will kill one person.

    What do you do?

    Would it make a difference to your decision if the single person was a child? Or others were old? Or if the five were children and the single old?

Would it make a difference if any of the people were members of your family? Would it make a difference if the five people were prisoners?

Would it make a difference if a single person was famous?

Consider your responses. Many people may decide that saving more people is better than just one person, but does this change if the identity of the one person is someone close to you? Or is there a difference in your decision making based on whether you must pull the lever, and thus the loss of life is a result of your action, versus not intervening… (although your inaction, it could be argued, is also an active decision)?

More tools are available in The Good Leadership Development Programme at www.goodleadership.org.

Relationship with Domain of Others (Mentor)

In the Dimension of Ethics, we have already explored the interdependence of the Inner Referee and Mentor. This interdependence manifests between Mentor and Custodian too. This gives a unique relationship between all three Characters within the Ethics Dimension. As you move outward, each Domain requires greater objectivity and universalism. There is a move from values to principles. The more clarity on these, the more confident Custodian can be. Custodian needs to be inclusive of others' beliefs whilst not compromising on their own. Holding on to deeply held values whilst safeguarding commonly accepted principles requires a depth of insight. Custodian gets both reference points and credibility from Mentor who in turn gets the same from Inner Referee.

Summary

Custodian ensures justice. It considers the wholesomeness of action and its impact on history, the present, and future generations. In an uncertain world, it provides an anchor for decision making. It determines the rightness of interventions into a system.

Custodian's key role is to provide a societal conscience and leave a positive legacy. It allows a safe space to answer difficult questions.

Custodian collaborates with the other three 'Domain of Context' Characters in the following ways:

1. Custodian gives Conductor an opportunity to spread goodness and influence positively.
2. Custodian gives Oracle deeper insights into a system. In particular, with reference to Ethical principles that govern the way things work and the moral consequences of interventions.
3. Custodian gives the Architect the steer to ensure its interventions leave a positive Ethical legacy and do not have negative impacts on the world.

ARCHITECT

Architect resides in the Domain of Context and the Dimension of Purpose.

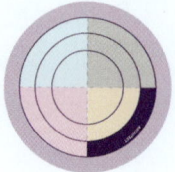

Who?

It builds new things that have relevance and sustainability for future generations. It puts in place structures and systems for addressing the big communal/societal questions. Architect thinks big and finds solutions. It builds bridges between previously separate elements.

Architect prototypes innovation. The talent of Architect is to lead from the perspective of a positively envisioned future. It can see a new world manifest before others. It relies on creativity, imagination, and possibilities.

Architect embraces change. Left on its own, it will break the rules and norms. In collaboration with Custodian however it builds a constructive future. It knows what needs to end so that the new can emerge. We see this pattern in nature; seasons change from summer to autumn, and we welcome the falling leaves as a sign that the trees are doing what they need. In organisations, we often get attached to what has gone before. Letting go of the past feels painful and we stem the flow of change. Architect is skilful at forcing and shaping the direction of change. With the influence of Custodian, it will respect what is ending and acknowledge history. It will thus keep healthy relations whilst still delivering its new agenda.

Working with Oracle, Architect would take a bird's eye, whole system approach to innovation. An Understanding of the materials at hand, their strengths, vulnerabilities, and purpose. Who are the best people to deliver the vision? Who in a team is flexible, adaptable, and able to reach out to others? Who may be more sceptical or resistant? What are the pressure points of the organisation? Who or what can bear a load and when? Architect's leadership role is to provide the inspiration and challenge that keep the vision community moving forward to achieving its collective goals.

Say and Do?

Motto: *'The future is bright, let's make it happen.'*

Architect not only dreams, but makes the dream a reality. It is persistent in building structures that affect and influence the many, not just a few. Architect brings the team together, the community that delivers a positive image of the future. It is the vision, strategy and action plan rolled into one. It enables people to see their place in the offered future. It sees possibilities and is optimistic that what is being built is desired. Architect believes that the new will be stronger and better than what went before. This gives Architect the confidence to break the rules and craft new systems. It is a spirited, can-do Character and inspires the same in others.

Portrait

Architect thinks about and paints a picture of a positive future for all. It lays out a pathway that shows how current action can be directed towards achieving this future. In doing so, it not only shapes the future but delivers it.

Benjamin Zander is the music director of the Boston Philharmonic Youth Orchestra, a youth orchestra composed of both high school and college aged students. He brings Architect to the fore when teaching music to children who are not achieving at school. They have little aspiration or connection to a positive sense of their own futures or their role in a wider one. Zander has a very powerful practice for his students. In the first lesson of the semester, he tells them all that they already have an A grade for this class. What he requires of them is to write a letter from the future telling him what they did to get the A grade. This letter is shared with their classmates. It is a straightforward positive visualisation that has powerful results. It also builds a vision community in the class, helping one another to achieve. As an Architect, he enables the students to gather around a commonality. They are no longer wasting energy in competition or comparisons with one another. He gets them to work together, as an orchestra would, to achieve a positive image of the future. Everyone has a responsibility for this common future.

In Shakespeare's play 'The Tempest', the positive vision of the Architect is embodied when Miranda observes:

O' wonder! How many goodly creatures are there here! How beauteous mankind is! O brave new world, that has such people in't.

Miranda's father, Prospero puts his Architect to work through engineering the marriage of Ferdinand and Miranda. He gets them to fall in love to restore power and overcome the darker forces that are part of the island's life.

In a more contemporary film, Nelson Mandela's Architect in action is portrayed in 'Invictus.' The story is about his vision for South Africa (Peace and Reconciliation), creating the Rainbow Nation, and winning the Rugby World Cup. His concern is not only for historically abused black South Africans, but everyone, regardless of colour, lest a repeat of historic abuses occurs. He is mindful of not throwing the baby out with the bathwater and ensures his wider vision of a united South Africa is not derailed due to short sighted revenge or ill-considered policies.

See: Invictus in Good Leadership Book Movie Clips at: https://www.youtube.com/c/goodleadership/playlists

Architect and Leadership

Everything is subject to change. That is the nature of dynamic systems and beings. At their best, Architect works with Oracle, Custodian and Conductor to create a positive vision of the future in which ownership is shared. It builds on the Understanding of the Oracle, looking beyond what is, to what can be. It explores what needs to be uncovered for something new to emerge which may require shedding the current and historic thinking of the Oracle. It then uses the Custodian to ensure the new thinking is congruent with values and principles. It then relies on the Conductor to disseminate this new thinking and help motivate others to join the Architect on this new venture. In the Truth & Reconciliation processes used in South Africa, this was clearly understood as a key component in the formation of a new stable society. Nelson Mandela expresses Architect in his statement about the importance of hope and optimism:

> *"I am fundamentally an optimist. Whether that comes from nature or nurture, I cannot say. Part of being optimistic is keeping one's head pointed toward the sun, one's feet moving forward. There were many dark moments when my faith in humanity was surely tested, but I would not and could not give myself up to despair."*

In a post Covid world, many organisations need such thinking. What old practices need rethinking to make them relevant to the new realities? It is not uncommon for a commitment to change to emerge from adversity and difficult times.

Growing Up as Architect

You are concerned with making an impact and change for your whole community. You look for trends and solutions that are future proof. You challenge the status quo and look at the big picture. You assemble people who can facilitate, catalyse, and execute the change with you. You constantly scope the horizon and map out action and consequence. You are a dynamic change maker.

The mature Architect will have Depth in their Character. This is achieved through the 4Ls of development: Learn, Love, Lead and Live. Assess your Architect through reflecting on the statements in the table.

Score yourself based on:		
1 = Never; 2 = Sometimes; 3 = Most of the time; 4 = Always		
LEARN	*I understand what needs to change for success in an organisation/ system*	
LOVE	*I have a genuine passion and concern for successful change in society*	
LEAD	*I am active in creating change for a new society*	
LIVE	*I am a societal or organisational change-maker*	

If you score 2 or below on any of the above, this is an area of development for you. Reflect using the guides below:

- **Learn: Have a good understanding of what is needed for future success in an organisation/community/system.** Know that standing still will only move you backwards. You are interested in emerging issues that will become trends in the future. You study the process of innovation, community evolution, and organisational development.

- **Love: Have a genuine passion and concern for successful change in society.** You enjoy listening to the words different people use to describe their connection to the mission, Purpose, or future. You are passionate about the direction of travel of the organisation or community. You are comfortable in uncertainty and flourish when exploring new opportunities.

- **Lead: Active in creating change for a new society.** You connect to a vision community. You plan, articulate, and execute the future you want to see. You identify who can help and motivate them to join you. You plan your strategy, milestones, and success indicators. You champion and empower the innovators, change-makers, and visionaries. You paint a positive image of the future and inspire people to achieve it.

- **Live: You are a societal or organisational changemaker.** You dream big and make the dream a reality. Your attention and focus remain on the future. You know what needs to be done and how to get it delivered. You are a driving force and inspiration for others to emulate and follow.

A tool for exploring Architect: Emerging Issues:

An emerging issue is an event or phenomenon with the potential to have significant impact just over the horizon. These include things like satellites, climate change, genetic engineering, robotics, blockchain, AI etc.

1. Spend some time searching through social media and see what is being discussed around emerging issues and new trends.
2. Identify one of the issues
3. Draw a mind map showing the first order impact. i.e. What will this issue / change directly impact?

4. Continue the mind map showing second order impacts. i.e. If the change above was to happen, what next, what would this then impact on?
5. Continue to the third order impact based on the changes identified in 4 above too.
6. Consider social, economic, political, environmental, technological, legal, and spiritual impacts.

What do you, your organisation and your community need to do to prepare for these changes?

More tools are available in The Good Leadership Development Programme at www.goodleadership.org.

Relationship with Domain of Others (Navigator)

In the Dimension of Purpose, we have already explored how Navigator may be fulfilling a need of the Inner Visionary. In a similar way, Navigator also fulfils the need of Architect. The realisation of an organisational or societal vision needs people. This is the vision community. This community is nurtured through Navigator who identifies how others fit into a larger vision that Architect creates. Who is aligned and who is not? Working together, Navigator and Architect are a powerful combination for change and development. Architect creates possibilities for Navigator to take advantage of, for the sake of others. Whilst Navigator provides the inspired workforce to make the larger vision a reality.

Summary

Architect envisions a sustainable future and ensures a vision community can rally around it. In a volatile world, it provides direction and motivation. It proactively moves the system towards a positive change, ensuring relevance, creativity, and innovation. Its key role is to lead change in organisations and society. Architect collaborates with the other three 'Domain of Context' Characters in the following ways:

- Architect gives Conductor the opportunity to motivate and inspire whole communities into action.

- Architect allows Oracle to see futures for its system, based on intuition and opportunity, not just precedence and experience.
- Architect allows Custodian to shape a positive future that leaves a constructive and wholesome legacy.

CONDUCTOR

Custodian resides in the Domain of Context and the Dimension of Ethics.

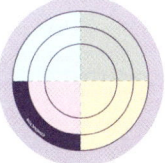

Who?

It has clarity about high-level and widespread messaging. It brings a sense of harmony of expression to the whole. Conductor ensures that each element of the system knows its role, entrances, and exits. It ensures key messages are highlighted, repeated, and illustrated across all platforms.

Conductor is like the leader of an orchestra - bringing out the expertise of the individual players to synchronise their joint effort for the best possible impact. Another meaning of Conductor is as a substance which carries an electrical charge. Conductivity is the capacity to transmit something, such as electricity or heat. So, we can say that the leadership roles of Conductor are two-fold:

1. To harmonise the voice of the parts to the whole.
2. To generate conductivity in a system. Ensuring messages are transmitted to its people, customers, and stakeholders.

Communication can be used for good or for evil. The meaning of Communication is the response it elicits – thus, the words we use profoundly impact thoughts, feelings, and actions. As such, Conductor has a critical role in leadership in that it can broadcast positively or negatively. Working with developed Oracles, Custodians and Architects it can influence many to move towards an optimistic future.

Social media is a powerful Conductor platform. A competent Conductor would master such media, both new and old. Used well, it can spread messages of peace, share the good news, connect people, advertise services, promote business, educate, and inform. But such platforms have been under attack because of the potential of misuse too. The gathering and abuse of big data, the dissemination of fake news, the interference with the processes of democracy, and the spread of hateful messages. The alliance of Conductor and Custodian would ensure that use of these media platforms is fair and proper.

Each epoch has had its respective Conductor platforms. Leaders used letter writing to invite treaties with neighbours, book writing to spread ideologies and propaganda, films/posters/radio broadcasts to assist the winning of wars even. Taking control of media platforms is often also the first act of civil uprising.

Conductor completes our set of Twelve Good Leadership Characters. When all the others are in place, Conductor enables messages of Understanding, Purpose, and Ethics to influence widely.

Say and Do?

Motto: *'Let's spread the word'*

The power of some social media influencers is testimony to the dangers of competency as a Conductor when the message is not wholesome. Conductor thus works best when other leadership Characters are in place. Conductor transmits messages and will make sure they are received and heard as intended. Repetition, repetition, repetition is a mantra of a working Conductor. Good timing is also a key talent of Conductor. Knowing when to send a message so that it can resonate at an optimal frequency mitigates the danger of a message being taken out of context. A challenge Conductor understands well.

Portrait

Conductor accurately predicts how a message will affect an audience. It knows the right route to reach the right people. It thus has a flexibility of approach. It will highlight different aspects and use different routes to get to different people. It knows how to tailor a message for the greatest transmission and impact. It will grasp the 'conductivity' of the platform as much as the effectiveness of the message on that specific platform. For example, a Twitter (X) message requires a different use of language to a Blog. Facebook has a different audience than Instagram. The right use of a #hashtag, an image, a video, a meme, or a link will result in a wider reach. Conductors take all opportunities open to them to spread the word and increase their influence.

Through his plays, we have seen how Shakespeare himself was a master Conductor. His stage was a 'mirror to nature' and a platform to Communicate widely the affairs of the state and the heart - the public and private worlds of those who govern and are governed.

> *All the world's a stage, and all the men and women merely players; they have their exits and their entrances, and one man in his time plays many parts, his acts being seven ages. (As You Like It)*

With a timeless resonance, he enthralled audiences using comedy, tragedy and history - from his Globe Theatre four centuries ago, to audiences across the globe today. Some scholars consider his final play, 'The Tempest,' as a personal retirement message. Shakespeare, through the character of Prospero, relinquishes his powers for a quieter, humbler, and human-sized existence. In this play, Shakespeare is telling us that Conductors have great power. This power must be used to serve the joy and fulfilment of others and not be an end in itself.

A contemporary, albeit controversial, Conductor can be seen in the film 'Social Network.' The Facebook founder, Mark Zuckerberg, is portrayed here as a Conductor at work, but without a developed Inner Advisor or Inner Referee. It shows the power of competency as a Conductor. However, shadows can also emerge if the Inner Domains of Leadership (in this case, Inner Advisor and Inner Referee) are undeveloped. Mark develops a tool that disseminates and connects with people in a way hitherto unknown. He tunes into the needs of billions of social media users. He speaks their language and connects those with a common interest. His character, however, is not always in tune with the voices in his own head, nor able to effectively Communicate well with those immediately around him. Without the influence of a developed Inner Referee, you go on to see the character betraying the trust of friends and colleagues in the pursuit of his vision and influence.

See: The Social Network in Good Leadership Book Movie Clips at: https://www.youtube.com/c/goodleadership/playlists

Conductor and Leadership

Conductor, the outward-facing communicator, features strongly in traditional models of leadership. The paradigm is strong leaders have strong opinions. They are good at letting others know what they stand for. This is true, but incomplete for Good Leadership. For example, let's take elections that are often fought on only these grounds. Promises are made with little regard for their actual viability or truth. In this way, the leadership Dimension of Communication is exploited and warped to the point that it starts to undermine the very nature of wholesome leadership. In leadership, once promises are made, followers expect them to be kept. A holistic approach to leadership, one that ensures the importance of all Twelve Characters, is thus essential.

Conductor in 21st century leadership is no more or less prominent than in the past. Yet, mastering and using it well is even more critical for leaders today. As a society, we are very new to conducting leadership messages on the scale we can today. The power of such wide-ranging platforms and reach needs coupling with integrity, intelligence, and positive intent. A humble awareness of the influence at one's fingertips. A precise, well-placed message can bring integration and harmony, or disagreement and division.

Growing up as Conductor

You broadcast your message far and wide, to the whole community. You are consistent across multiple platforms and adopt new ones as they emerge. You have reach and you deliver impactful messages across demographics. You recognise new trends and conversations. You track impact and adapt to increase influence further. You resonate with the public.

The mature Conductor will have Depth in their Character. This is achieved through the 4Ls of development: Learn, Love, Lead and Live. Assess your Conductor by reflecting on the statements in the table.

Score yourself based on:		
1 = Never; 2 = Sometimes; 3 = Most of the time; 4 = Always		
LEARN	*I understand Communication and media platforms*	
LOVE	*I am uplifted by harmony with the wider world*	
LEAD	*I am confident and comfortable with multi- platform Communication*	
LIVE	*I am tuned into my organisation, society, and the world around me*	

If you score 2 or below on any of the above, this is an area of development for you. Reflect using the guides below:

- **Learn: Have a good understanding of Communication and media platforms.** You have your finger on the pulse of what is current and trending. You take an interest in what is new and catch people's interest. You constantly seek new opportunities and mechanisms to reach out to wider communities.

- **Love: You are uplifted by harmony with the wider world.** You enjoy engaging and Communicating with people. You take pleasure in seeing your message spread far, and are excited by the potential of its impact. You are passionate about influencing people from across different demographics, and comfortable with adapting messages to resonate better with them.

- **Lead: You are confident and comfortable with multi-platform Communications.** You plan and execute the delivery of messaging competently. You identify and leverage all possible platforms, new and old. You have a comprehensive Communication strategy. You have a network that relays and amplifies your influence further. You are clear and effective in achieving the desired impact.

- **Live: You are tuned in to your organisation, society, and the world around you.** You reach people naturally and widely. People follow you because you resonate with them. You are an influencer. You know what needs to be said, where it needs to be said, and how it needs to be said.

A tool for exploring Conductor: Communicating across archetypes.

Conductor is required to Communicate across varying platforms and varied audiences. Conductor's strength is in communicating effectively in ways that connect to people of differing personality preferences. Personality types need to be considered to ensure messages are received. Most people have a preference towards receiving messages in the style of one or other of these four archetypal personalities: Good King, Guardian (or Great Mother), Artist and Warrior. Their energies also fuel the different Dimensions of Leadership, and thus, their appreciation and consideration help to better facilitate messages. Conductor needs to consider all personalities to ensure the widest possible dissemination of the correct message:

Good King: Fuels the Leadership Dimension of Understanding. The Good King is steadfast and rational. It has masculine static energy and in nature, is aligned with 'earth'. They are neutral, reasoned, have a steady gaze, and take their time and space - not too much, not too little. They listen and are listened to, Understand and are understood. They are strategic and thoughtful. Messages thus need to be considered, logical and structured. Develop your Good King energy by playing tactical games such as Chess or Cluedo. Practice chairing meetings and assembling opinions. Study mathematics and logic.

Guardian: Fuels the Leadership Dimension of Ethics. The Guardian is nurturing and caring. It has a feminine static energy and, in nature, is aligned with 'water.' It has a still and calm presence. With a focus on the other, it radiates warmth and compassion. It has a gentleness in voice and gesture. It is attractive and draws people in. It is reassuring and trust-building. Messages thus need to be gentle, warm, and conciliatory. Develop your Guardian energy by taking relaxing walks. Try meditation or yoga. Be still and quiet.

Artist: Fuels the Leadership Dimension of Purpose. The Artist is creative and innovative. It has a feminine dynamic energy and in nature, is aligned with 'air.' The signature of Artists is not in what they do but in how intense their motivation is to manifest the extraordinary. It inspires others. Artist generates, is passionate about, and is open to ideas. Its enthusiasm is infectious. Messages thus need to be imaginative, visionary and future focused. Develop your Artist energy by trying something new, maybe ballet or pottery! Read a poem or try creative writing. Use arts and crafts materials to build something you have never tried.

Warrior: Fuels the Leadership Dimension of Communication. The Warrior is rousing and motivating. It has masculine dynamic energy and, in nature, is aligned with 'fire.' It is linked to invincibility and strength. The power to protect, project and defend. It is happy on the front line, speaking out and taking action. It is confident, firm, expansive, posed and forward moving. Messages thus need to be stimulating, stirring, and exciting. Develop your Warrior energy by trying competitive sports. Have a go at karate or a punching bag. Work out in a gym or go climbing.

Use these various energies to resonate with different people and personalities.

More tools are available in The Good Leadership Development Programme at www.goodleadership.org.

Relationship with Domain of Others (Storyteller)

In the Dimension of Communication, we have already explored how Storyteller draws on Inner Advisor. In a similar way, Conductor draws on Storyteller and the three remain connected in this way. As you move to the outer Domains, the primary change is the number of recipients. The content is often the same and merely adapted for wider distribution. Leaders need Conductor to coordinate the spread of their message to others. Storyteller crafts the message for Conductor to disseminate.

Many leaders fail because they do not adapt to the changing mechanisms of 'conducting well'. With the ability to reach more and more people getting easier, a good Storyteller alone may no longer be adequate. In these days of personality-led influencers (Conductors), it is important that people of good character, with a good story, learn how to Conduct themselves well. The use of online platforms has become critical to the success of spreading leadership messages.

Summary

Conductor is a mass Communication specialist. It uses language, images, and timing to influence others across many platforms. It relies on its inner Domains and other Dimensions for content. In an ambiguous world, it provides clarity. Its key role is to spread the leadership message far and wide. Conductor collaborates with the other three 'Domain of Context' Characters in the following ways:

- Conductor gives Oracle the Communication tools that allow fuller leveraging of networks.
- Conductor gives Custodian the mechanisms to spread its message of goodness, and positively impact the world.
- Conductor gives Architect the platforms to sell its vision, and build a wider vision community.

CHAPTER 3
LEVELLING UP AND JOINING UP

"You can do what I cannot do. I can do what you cannot do. Together we can do great things."

Mother Teresa

LEVELLING UP AND JOINING UP

The Good Leadership Model requires you to develop all Twelve Characters. As you Learn, Love, Lead and Live each one, your positive potential increases. Not just because of the skills each brings, but how they combine to release even more value. The Characters synergise to produce a joint result greater than the sum of their individual efforts. Working alone, they are smart, working in tandem, they are brilliant.

Levelling Up to become Specialists

We have already introduced how the Characters interact with one another within each Dimension. How the Inner Advisor supports the Storyteller, which informs the Conductor. How the Inner Master enables the Empath, which assists the Oracle. How the Inner Referee legitimises the Mentor which does the same for the Custodian. How Inner Visionary inspires the Navigator which garners support for the Architect. Developing all the Characters within each Dimension in this way allows you to 'level up' and become a Specialist in that Dimension of Good Leadership - an Understanding Specialist, an Ethical Specialist, a Purpose Specialist, or a Communication Specialist. Each Specialist is the combined attributes of the Characters from the three different Domains within that Dimension. They inform and support one another to boost their effectiveness. These Specialists are categorised as either Grounding or Growth. The Specialists of Grounding are Understanding and Ethics. They have a foundational role upon which leadership can be built. The Specialists of Growth are Purpose and Communication. They have an enhancing role in creating and facilitating change.

Understanding Specialist

The three Characters in the Dimension of Understanding are the Inner Master, Empath and Oracle. As you develop all three, you will 'level up' to become the Understanding Specialist.

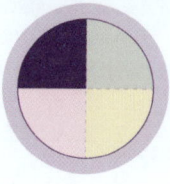

> *"I catch the pattern of your silence before you speak, I do not need to hear a word. In your silence every tone I seek is heard."*
>
> **Silence by Langston Hughes**

It possesses the static masculine energy of the archetypal Good King. It is authoritative, strategic, commanding, and structured. As both grounding and foundational, the Understanding Specialist provides insights into context, analyses strengths, identifies weaknesses, and mitigates against risks. It grasps the seen and senses the unseen as one would expect from a Master, Empath, and Oracle.

Profile of the Understanding Specialist:

	Inner Master	Empath	Oracle
Learn	Understands personal frames of reference	Understands others' frames of reference	Understands contextual frames of reference
Love	Accepting of self	Passionate about engaging others	Marvels in complexity
Lead	Practices personal presence	Relatable with others	Connects to and leverages stakeholders
Live	Confident and comfortable with self	Confident and comfortable with others	Confident and comfortable with complexity

Ethical Specialist

The three Characters in the Dimension of Ethics are the Inner Referee, Mentor and Custodian. As you develop all three, you will 'level up' to become the Ethical Specialist.

> *"How sweet is the shepherd's sweet lot! From the morn to the evening he strays; he shall follow his sheep all the day, and his tongue shall be filled with praise. For he hears the lambs' innocent call, and he hears the ewes' tender reply; he is watchful while they are in peace, for they know when their shepherd is night."*
> **The Shepherd by William Blake**

It possesses the static feminine energy of the archetypal Guardian or Great Mother. It is caring, radiates warmth, and is inviting and generous. In common with the Understanding Specialist, it is both grounding and foundational. The Ethical Specialist provides insights into right and wrong, provides a principled paradigm for decision-making, and prioritises sustainability. Its presence is reassuring and supportive, as one would expect from a Referee, Mentor and Custodian.

Profile of the Ethical Specialist:

	Inner Referee	**Mentor**	**Custodian**
Learn	Understands personal values and morals	Understands the rights and values of others	Understands the law and principles
Love	Uplifted	Passionate about the moral development of others	Nurturing and taking responsibility
Lead	Walks the talk, whistleblows, and makes a stand	Takes an interest in the well-being of others	Upholds the law, and is in service to others and society
Live	Has moral integrity and authenticity	Respects and is respected	Has a sustained commitment to the success of communities and the planet

Purpose Specialist

The three Characters in the Dimension of Purpose are the Inner Visionary, Navigator and Architect. As you develop all three, you will 'level up' to become the Purpose Specialist.

> *"Life is real! Life is earnest! And the grave is not its goal; dust thou art, to dust returnest, was not spoken of the soul. Not enjoyment, and not sorrow, is our destined end or way; but to act, that each tomorrow find us farther than today."*
>
> **A Psalm of Life by Henry Wadsworth Longfellow**

It possesses the dynamic feminine energy of the archetypal Artist. It is vibrant, creative, visionary, and innovative. As both growth and enhancing, the Purpose Specialist is the changemaker, thinks out of the box, is disruptive, and takes a longer-term view. It sets direction and acts as a beacon towards a better future, as would a Visionary, Navigator and Architect.

Profile of the Purpose Specialist:

	Inner Visionary	Navigator	Architect
Learn	Has conscious intentions and life's journey planned	Sees value in the vision of others	Has a good understanding of what is needed for the future
Love	Has joy in engaging with the journey	Takes a genuine interest in the vision of others	Has a genuine passion and concern for the success of society
Lead	Is brave in experiencing what is new and stepping into the unknown	Guides, facilitates, and capacity builds others to achieve their fullest potential	Is active in creating a better society
Live	Is driven, determined, and focused	Is a consummate helper and door-opener	A societal or organisational change-maker

Communication Specialist

The three Characters in the Dimension of Communication are the Inner Advisor, Storyteller and Conductor. As you develop all three, you will 'level up' to become the Communication Specialist.

> *"From harmony, from heavenly harmony, this universal frame began: when nature underneath a heap of jarring atoms lay, and could not heave her head, the tuneful voice was heard from high, 'Arise, ye more than dead!' Then cold, and hot, and moist, and dry, In order to their stations leap, and Music's power obey."*
>
> **A Song for St. Cecilia's Day by John Dryden**

It possesses the dynamic masculine energy of the archetypal Warrior. It is assertive, powerful, and impactful. In common with the Purpose Specialist, it is both growth and enhancing. The Communication Specialist is motivating, ensures action, and rallies others to the cause. It rouses through harmonising messages, thus allowing them to penetrate the heart, body, mind, and spirit – as one would expect from an Advisor, Storyteller and Conductor.

Profile of the Communication Specialist:

	Inner Advisor	Storyteller	Conductor
Learn	Recognises and understands their inner voice	Aware of the impact narratives have on others	Has a good understanding of communication and media platforms
Love	Is centred and enjoys self-talk	Takes pleasure in interacting with others	Uplifted by harmony with the wider world
Lead	Reflects well	Articulate and relatable	Confident and comfortable with multi-platform communications
Live	Tuned in to self	Tuned in to others	Tuned in to organisation, society, and the world

Joining Up Specialists to release Virtue Practitioners

The collaboration of two Specialists reveals a Leadership Virtue. Aristotle describes virtue as a positive character developed through habituation. That is, doing the right thing over and over. As such, for the Leadership Virtue to emerge, you must fully Learn, Love, Lead and Live the two combined Specialists. Make them a habit such that they become your default behaviours, and you are trusted by those around you, your followers, to act in this way.

Six Characters, three from each of the two combined Dimensions, act together to release each Leadership Virtue. By combining Specialisms, the Characters from each are then endowed with the added value of these Leadership Virtues. The sum being greater than the parts.

These Leadership Virtues we describe as Prudent, Wise, Social, Just, Spiritual and Courageous. When Specialists of any two Dimensions combine, we are saying that the person now becomes a Practitioner of that Leadership Virtue or a Virtue Practitioner.

- **A PRUDENT PRACTITIONER** is both an Understanding and Ethical Specialist
- **A WISE PRACTITIONER** is both an Understanding and Purpose Specialist
- **A SOCIAL PRACTITIONER:** is both an Understanding and Communication Specialist
- **A JUST PRACTITIONER:** is both a Communication and Ethical Specialist
- **A SPIRITUAL PRACTITIONER:** is both a Purpose and Ethical Specialist
- **A COURAGEOUS PRACTITIONER:** is both a Purpose and Communication Specialist.

Let's now look at the dynamics involved in becoming a Virtue Practitioner and how this insight also reveals the negative potential of under-developed Specialists. These negative potentials are either Leadership Vices or Blind Spots. A Leadership Vice is when both Specialists are under-developed. A Blind Spot is when one Specialist dominates without the support of the other. We can all manifest shadows at times, but we must acknowledge them and learn from our shortcomings. Doing what it takes to better develop the Characters and Specialists that are weak and led to the manifestation of the shadow. As leaders, however, it is also important to remember that the ripple effect of positive or negative decisions can be felt for years. As such, leaders must own their mistakes and ensure the mitigation of their consequences.

The Prudent Practitioner

Prudent Practitioners are Specialists in Understanding and Ethics. This combination provides emotional intelligence and a depth of insight, coupled with a foundation for positive action and intent. Each Specialist enhances the other to reveal the Leadership Virtue of Prudence.

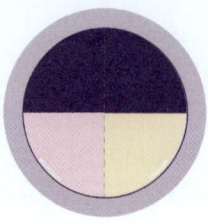

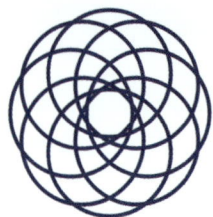 

The mastery of self, others and context are applied towards moral problem-solving. Reason and logic are used in a disciplined and fair way. **The Prudent Practitioner understands risk and applies the appropriate Ethical care.** Steadfastness, guidance, and responsibility are applied whilst seeking relevant solutions in a system. Morality is used in a contextually applicable way. **The Prudent Practitioner protects what is Ethically right but champions it with Understanding.** Decisions and judgments are sound and withstand scrutiny. Solutions are acceptable and based on precedence and principle. Governance and due diligence are prioritised.

Prudent Inner Master and Inner Referee

In the Domain of Self, Inner Master gives the Inner Referee insight into the personal effects of Ethical positions; and Inner Referee gives Inner Master its conscience. In combination, the Prudent Practitioner of the Domain of Self is both resilient and resolute.

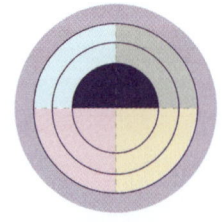

Impulses are controlled. Morality is applied with a consideration of how it affects oneself. Why values are important is understood. Choices are practical and pragmatic. Shortcomings are mitigated against and forgiven too.

Prudent Empath and Mentor

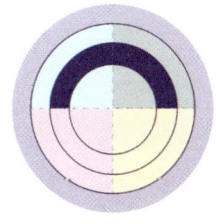

In the Domain of Others, Empath gives Mentor insight into the effect of its Ethical positions on others; and Mentor gives Empath the opportunity to explore the diversity of morality others bring. In combination, the Prudent Practitioner of the Domain of Others can both pace and direct. Interactions are meaningful and relatable.

Values-based interventions consider where the other is in their leadership journey. Moral dilemmas that others are facing are understood. Guidance is relevant and timely. Plans are tailor-made, success celebrated, and failure supported.

Prudent Oracle and Custodian

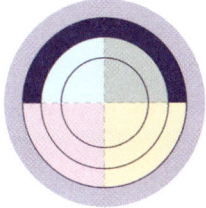

In the Domain of Context, Oracle gives Custodian insight into how to positively impact the wider system; and Custodian gives Oracle the opportunity to explore the moral consequences of interventions. In combination, the Prudent Practitioner of the Domain of Context is respected and respectful. Trusted and trust-giving.

Interventions are grounded, principled, and informed. The direction is set to leave a positive legacy based on organisational capability. Challenges are forecasted, risks assessed, scenarios planned, and principled approaches for implementation sought. Growth is sustainable and encourages partnerships. Networks are both leveraged and supported. Relationships are sought with those sharing values, and collaborations lead to mutual gain.

The Prudent Practitioner in Action

One way to spot a Prudent Practitioner is in the way Human Resources are run in an organisation. The way that people join and leave an organisation, or are treated during grievances and disciplinaries. Do processes meet the needs of both people and organisation with dignity and respect? Or are people treated as objects and commodities? What processes are in place for an employee to be their best selves at work? Do people leave well? A Prudent Practitioner will review, explore and adapt to the specifics of a situation. They would not be content with a 'one size fits all' approach to handling people. Recruits will be valued and respected. Both skills and needs are assessed. Benefits and risks are considered. Joint responsibility is taken for the success of individuals and teams. Fairness is sought – not just because it is right for the individual but for the long-term running of the organisation too. A Prudent Practitioner is not a rash decision-maker. Credibility is more important than speed. This may lead to actions which run contrary to what others may feel are obvious. Decisions will then be criticised or challenged. That is, until something goes wrong. Then you will hear people say, "thank goodness we did that!"

Prudence is a Virtue which, unfortunately, is appreciated more through hindsight. To see Prudence in action, it is well worth looking at the late Robin Cook's resignation speech to the UK Parliament in 2003. Robin Cook MP was part of the Cabinet at the time that Britain was embarking on a war with Iraq. He was reported to be one of the Cabinet's chief opponents of military action. On 17 March 2003, he resigned from the Cabinet. As you listen to his speech, you hear both an Ethical Specialist, calling for what is right, and an Understanding Specialist, calling for more information and insight before acting. He shares that there was no way of estimating the potential loss of civilian life, and that there was no evidence of a humanitarian crisis to which the international community had a duty to respond. In his statement giving his reasons for resigning, he said:

> *"I can't accept collective responsibility for the decision to commit Britain now to military action in Iraq without international agreement or domestic support… The reality is that Britain is being asked to embark on a war without agreement in any of the international bodies of which we are a leading partner –not NATO, not the European Union and, now, not the (UN) Security Council."*
> *"Our interests are best protected not by unilateral action but by multilateral agreement and a world order governed by rules."*

Shadows of Prudent Practitioners:

Leadership Vice: Blundering

Blind Spots: Naïve and Mischievous

The Leadership Vice of Blundering results from a lack of Understanding and Ethics. A complete absence of these components of Prudence leads to carelessness and insensitivity. Actions are taken without due thought and consideration. They are tactless, reckless, misjudged, and irresponsible.

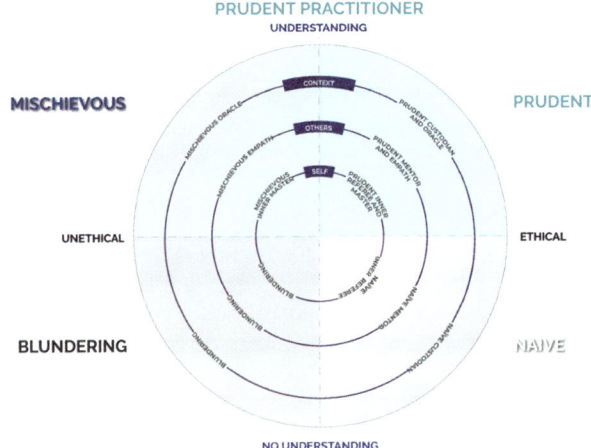

The Blind Spots result from the lack of either Understanding or Ethics. The absence of Understanding (but with Ethics) leads to the Blind Spot of Naive. Actions are well intended but lack insight into the actual realities of a situation. This naivety can be taken advantage of by others. It leaves institutions such as justice, religion and armed forces open to abuse.

The absence of Ethics (but with Understanding) leads to the Blind Spot of Mischievous. Systemic knowledge is abused for illicit gain. Information and networks are misappropriated. The naivety mentioned above is exploited.

Place yourself into this scenario: You lead a hospital team and need to raise finances to buy the latest state-of-the-art technology for your department. You need to consider where the money comes from; what is promised in return for any donation; whether the equipment is being purchased at the best price; the impact of purchasing or not; and other priorities or demands upon resources. You might wish to hear from the families of patients who could benefit from the new technology, or research other options to explore the longevity of the investment.

Ask yourself the questions: Would you be driven solely by personal values? Perhaps to save a single life is all the justification needed? Would you look primarily at your role as head of the department? Your duty of care towards those in your team as well as the patients on the waiting list. If so, then you may have chosen to turn a blind eye to the potential that there might be more aspects of this decision to consider. You may operate Naively. High Ethics/Low Understanding.

Or, you may have a high Understanding of the impact of obtaining this new equipment. Aware of the benefits to individuals and families, as well as the kudos it would bring to your department. You may know that this is exactly what you have been waiting for. An opportunity to demonstrate your leadership capabilities. You get straight into negotiations with one of the lead suppliers. You tell your team that you have researched all the other options - though in fact you haven't. Instead, you have developed a unique relationship with the supplier. You tie your department into a pricey maintenance contract for the next five years. In return, the supplier guarantees that they will not supply the same equipment to other hospitals within a hundred-mile radius. This is Mischievous behaviour. High Understanding/Low Ethics.

Finally, imagine in this scenario your attention is distracted by other things. You rush to publicise the news about the equipment before planning how it will be sourced, paid for, or a timeline for implementation. Your team and stakeholders may be uplifted for a short while, but there is no strategy to fulfil promises. Sooner or later, people will start to ask when, how, and what questions. People rarely notice that they are 'Blundering around,' but others notice it.

Blundering comes with connotations of clumsy, insensitive and careless. Note - David Cameron acted Blundering when he called the UK referendum on Europe in 2016. He was a supporter of staying in

Europe. He intended to appease Eurosceptics in his party, it was not what he personally believed was right for the country. He had little Understanding of the mood of the country or complexity of such a question. Whether you supported remain or leave, the calling for the referendum with such a lack of Understanding and integrity is Blundering. The consequence was the messy history of 'Getting Brexit Done.'

Whilst possessing the Leadership Vice of Blundering, you are unable to 'level up' to any of the other Virtue Practitioners except Courage (which requires Purpose and Communication only). As such, it is possible to be a Courageous Practitioner and be Blundering.

To avoid these leadership shadows and become a Prudent Practitioner, there must be a conscious choice to have an active and equal dialogue between the Specialists of Understanding and Ethics. Both are Grounding Specialists. They both possess static energies and have foundational properties. Collaboration thus has little tension.

As we progress through the other Practitioners, it is worth keeping in mind that a complete leader must be competent in all the Specialists and thus, all the Leadership Virtues. This, of course, is a matter of development, opportunity, skill, and application. Learn, Love, Lead and Live.

The Wise Practitioner

Wise Practitioners are Specialists in Understanding and Purpose. This combination provides deep insight, and the inspiration needed to leverage it for the future. Each Specialist enhances the other to reveal the Leadership Virtue of Wisdom.

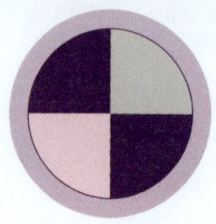

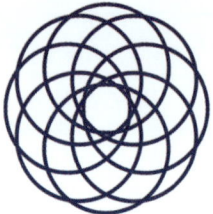 

The mastery of self, others, and context are used to move towards preferred goals. **The Wise Practitioner not only knows how something works but is also open-minded to its innovative applications.** The Wise Practitioner Understands what is happening and uses this knowledge to achieve Purpose. Sound judgment and discernment are accompanied by curiosity and imagination. Advancement is astutely considered alongside available resources. A future is built, allowing for ground realities. **The Wise Practitioner drives towards the desired Purpose but Understands risk, mitigation, and challenges.** Problems are solved through investigation of 'what is' and 'what can be.' Wise Practitioners thus provide counsel to others with a superior level of perspective and are often seen as learned. Pleasure is taken in looking both deep and far. Self-interest is compromised in favour of the bigger picture.

Wise Inner Master and Inner Visionary

In the Domain of Self, Inner Master gives the Inner Visionary awareness that informs its journey; and Inner Visionary provides the Inner Master with intuitive insights. In combination, the Wise Practitioner of the Domain of Self is paradoxically both stable and flexible.

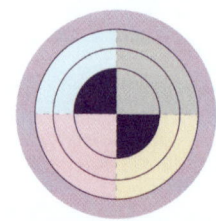

The personal impact of actions is considered. Internal limits are mitigated or transformed into assets for the future. Personal consequences of action or inaction are understood. Choices are constructive and valuable, building effectiveness and advancing ambition.

Wise Empath and Navigator

In the Domain of Others, Empath gives Navigator insight into the situation of others; and Navigator allows Empath to explore the passion of others. In combination, the Wise Practitioner of the Domain of Others can relate and arouse. Interactions are pertinent. Others are inspired based on both where they are, and where they  need to be. The direction allows for challenges others may face, and provides the tools and determination to overcome them. Guidance is both appropriate and motivational. Plans are focused on milestones and success indicators.

Wise Oracle and Architect

In the Domain of Context, Oracle gives Architect insight into how a system works; and Architect gives Oracle insight into opportunities. In combination, the Wise Practitioner of the Domain of Context is a change-maker extraordinaire. Einstein said, *"Knowledge defines all we currently know and understand. Imagination points to all we might yet* 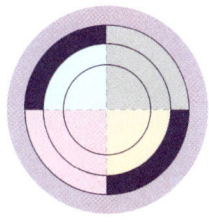 *discover and create."* The Wise Oracle and Architect are endowed with both, Understanding and imagination. Problems are addressed with a clear image of the future in mind. Interventions are 'realistically creative.' Growth is encouraged but also guided. Organisational history is acknowledged, yet change is embraced. Both vision and detailed strategy are crafted. Value creation is sought through collaboration, and connections are made to advance learning and progress.

The Wise Practitioner in action

All three Abrahamic faiths recognise King Solomon as a ruler famous for his Wisdom. Perhaps the best-known story of his Wisdom is the 'Judgment of Solomon.' Two women each lay claim to be the mother of the same child. Solomon resolves the dispute by commanding the child to be cut in half and shared between the two. One woman promptly renounces her claim. She would rather give the child up than see it killed. Solomon declares the woman who showed compassion is the true mother. Solomon's approach is innovative. Thankfully, only the imagination is used here to achieve the desired Purpose, and no one is actually physically injured. Yet, the awareness of the response and of a mother is also Understood in exercising this Wise strategy.

In 2015, Justin Trudeau, became the Prime Minister of Canada. He believed strongly that leaders must find a way of embracing diversity in their countries. In 2015 he appointed the first-ever cabinet of 15 men and 15 women. In 2018 he was quoted as saying, *"Any comment about how a man looks isn't even an eyelash worth of the systemic discrimination women face. As a man in business and politics, I had many advantages, and I didn't suffer the discrimination, sexism, superficiality, and judgment that women go through daily."* He took an opportunity at Davos to urge CEOs to promote more women to senior positions and adopt a zero-tolerance policy toward sexual harassment at work. He explained how curbing the gender gap in Canada would add $150 billion to its GDP by 2026. Prime Minister Trudeau shows a depth of Understanding of, not only the issue, but also what motivates the audience. He then uses this to move his country and those he influences towards the desired Purpose. He acts with the Leadership Virtue of Wisdom.

Shadows of Wise Practitioners:

Leadership Vice: Lost

Blind Spots: Excited and Despondent

The Leadership Vice of Lost results from the lack of both Understanding and Purpose. Decisions are made without full awareness or insight and without an eye on preferred outcomes. Situations are misread, and even well-intended actions can be ignorant. A complete absence of these components of Wisdom leads to doubt and confusion. Traumatised people can be in this state. When trauma happens, part of the memory function of the brain shuts down. It thus becomes very hard to access Understanding of a traumatic event to give it meaning and Purpose. People become Lost and bewildered. Patience, care, and a gentle unveiling of clarity are needed. The way out is a movement towards Understanding and meaning. This can be slow and painful. Sometimes we just have to wait for the fog to clear so a path can be found.

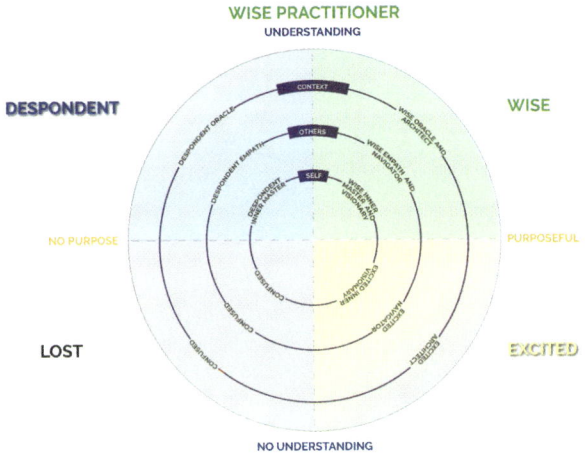

The Blind Spots result from the lack of either Understanding or Purpose. The absence of Understanding (but with Purpose) leads to the Blind Spot of Excited. Actions are intended to progress towards the desired outcome but without essential insights into present realities. Vision is not accompanied by sound strategy. Actions can be rash, and losses are incurred. Policy and process are ignored. Side effects or negative consequences are missed.

The absence of Purpose (but with Understanding) leads to the Blind Spot of Despondent. U-turns become commonplace. Missions are not aligned, and opportunities are missed. Growth can become frustrated by a lack of direction. Information and networks remain under-utilised, and actions can lose their meaning.

Place yourself into this scenario: You take on a new role. It provides you with an opportunity to deliver a project that is very close to your heart. A project that will benefit many people by providing a sanctuary from the stresses of urban living. A Public Gallery or a City Landscaping project, perhaps. Imagine a project that captures your imagination and tugs at your heartstrings.

You need to consider what the final vision for the project is. Who will use it? How do you ensure accessibility? What need is it satisfying? How can you make it stand out? Who will help you deliver it? What resources are needed? What is the timeline and project plan? How will you handle security? How to source sustainable components? What is needed to keep it relevant decades from now? How do you get the best value for money? Does your consultation need to be wider?

Ask yourself the question: Would you be driven solely by innovation and imagination? Perhaps making a statement is more important than anything else. If so, you run the risk of Excited behaviour. High Purpose/Low Understanding.

Or, you may have a high Understanding of the logistics required in delivering this project. Aware of the nuts and bolts of project management, risk, and mitigation. You begin putting pen to paper. You deposit money to secure suppliers even though you are still unsure of the final design. You secure labourers and professionals well in advance to avoid shortages over the holiday period. But the design changes over the months. This means engineers are delayed and workforces sit idle. An evolving vision means supplies remain unused, or storage becomes costly. This is Despondent behaviour: High Understanding/Low Purpose.

Finally, imagine in this scenario you focus on neither. Announcements are given to the public and media about the project with a made-up deadline. People hail you as a hero. But time reveals there is no realistic vision nor plan for the space. Reputations are damaged and money is misspent. The warning signs are often felt well in advance, but path dependency and being Lost as to what to do next leads to bankruptcy.

Being Lost comes with connotations of being out of one's depth, clueless, and incompetent. Creative and visionary projects need a Wise approach to bring them to fruition. The aborted Garden Bridge in

London, in 2017, shows Excited behaviour, which eventually impacts the original Purpose too, resulting in Lost. The original Architect of the idea was Joanna Lumley, who envisioned a "floating paradise" as a memorial to Princess Diana. The proposal was strongly supported and championed by the, then Mayor of London, Boris Johnson in 2013. Significant funds were expended on the project without a full Understanding of what was needed. These included costly publicity and galas. Costs had to be upwardly revised. Work halted and contractors were put on standby due to unsettled legal issues around land ownership. The Garden Bridge Trust ceased to be a going concern due to financial deficits. A review announced by the new Mayor, Sadiq Khan, was highly critical of the plan, its procurement, its cost, the risk to public funds, and value for money. The failed project cost £53 million, most of which was public money. Indeed, what started as an Excited Architect (low Understanding but with Purpose) eventually became Lost, as its Purpose became clouded with political and personal legacy ambitions. The Independent newspaper reported:

> *"Instead of a modern monument celebrating sustainability and public space, the failed bridge has become symbolic of political and economic recklessness… in its spectacular unravelling the bridge now offers us a masterclass in how not to achieve something. What seems to be central to the failure of the project was a profound lack of understanding about what the bridge would actually be or who it was for, let alone what the true costs of building the bridge and the annual maintenance charges would be. What started as a vision that would provide Londoners with a peaceful and tranquil way to cross the river Thames on foot, was fast being viewed as a way to privatise part of the Thames and make a personal stamp that would give Boris Johnson a lot of attention."*

Whilst possessing the Leadership Vice of Lost, you are unable to 'level up' to any of the other Virtue Practitioners except Just (which requires Ethics and Communication only). As such, it is possible to be a Just Practitioner and be Lost.

To avoid these leadership shadows and become a Wise Practitioner, there needs to be a conscious choice to have an active and equal dialogue between the Specialists of Understanding and Purpose. One possesses static energy whilst the other is dynamic. One is a Grounding

Specialist, and the other is a Growth Specialist. There can exist tension between them, as one encourages thought whilst the other prefers intuition.

The Social Practitioner

Social Practitioners are Specialists in Understanding and Communication. This combination allows them to know something well and articulate it just as well. Each Specialist enhances the other to reveal the Leadership Virtue of Social.

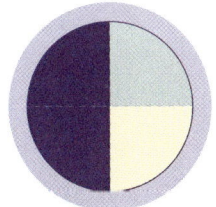

Another way to describe Social Practitioner would be Worldly Practitioners. Psychology, anthropology, economics, politics, and linguistics are their comfort areas. Emotional and social intelligence allow them to influence others and situations with ease. Connections are built and nurtured through nuanced, flexible, and responsive language. Messages are tailored and cultured. The Social Practitioner Understands what is happening around them and thus, how best to Communicate to influence. Listening, questioning, and exploring provide even more information to deepen insights. The Social Practitioner Communicates widely to further Understanding. This positive feedback loop allows continual learning and adaptability. Understanding informs Communication which feeds back to further Understanding. Building relationships and rapport comes naturally, allowing ease to get along with and tensions to be diffused.

Social Inner Master and Inner Advisor

In the Domain of Self, both Inner Master and Inner Advisor positively reinforce each other. In combination, the Social Practitioner of the Domain of Self is a perpetual learner. Internal dialogue is constantly engaged. Strengths and weaknesses are known and reviewed. Thought precedes action and action precipitates further

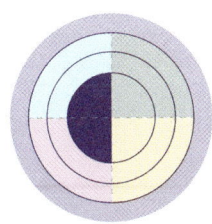

thought. Information is gathered, absorbed, processed, and used to better inform decision-making.

Social Empath and Storyteller

In the Domain of Others, Empath gives Storyteller insight into others to make a stronger impact; and Storyteller helps Empath get a deeper Understanding of others. In combination, the Social Practitioner of the Domain of Others can both relate and is relatable. Interactions are appropriately nuanced and flexible.

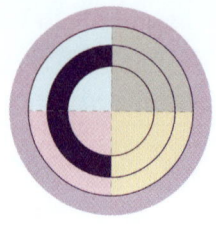

Showing up as needed; entertaining when an entertainer is required; comforting when a comforter is required; loving when a lover is required. Connections are made with people at different levels in an organisation. Inspiration is delivered through pacing and building rapport, using the right language to motivate action. Instructions are clear and objections handled through precise language based on an awareness of others.

Social Oracle and Conductor

In the Domain of Context, Oracle gives Conductor the insights needed to spread its message; and Conductor gives Oracle the ability to leverage networks better. In combination, the Social Practitioner of the Domain of Context is an expert worldly Practitioner. They Understand both organisational culture and strategy. 'The way

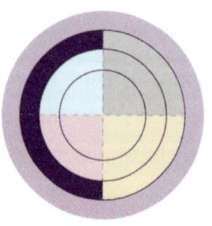

things operate around here' and how to influence it is understood. Direction is planned where needed and allowed to evolve unplanned where needed too. Wider networks are nurtured and used well. Branding and marketing are championed, and media platforms are connected to maintain the consistency of the message. Communication is segmented, tailored, and targeted to maximise reach and penetration.

The Social Practitioner in action

Martin Lewis, a media presenter and financial journalist, is an example of a Social Practitioner. He is a money-saving expert (MoneySavingExpert.com). He has a depth of Understanding as well as skills in Communicating with a wide audience. He has used radio, television, and digital/social media with great success. His academic studies at the London School of Economics and Cardiff School of Journalism gave him the Understanding needed in financial instruments/markets, and Communication platforms. Lewis was at the forefront of the media campaign to reclaim what he states are unfair and unlawful fees charged by UK banks. He championed the reclaiming of PPI that had been added to loans, credit card payments, and mortgages. In 2008, he appeared on television and radio exhorting consumers to 'cap your energy bills now.' This was based on the insightful prediction that there would be a further round of price increases at the end of 2008. Shortly afterwards, British Gas announced an increase of 30% on its uncapped prices. His influence and reach are extensive. His weekly emails are circulated wider than The New York Times Morning Briefing. He has over a million followers on Twitter (X) alone. His Oracle gives him deep insight into issues and how to solve them. His Empath means he cares for consumers, especially those most affected. His Inner Master allows him to keep composure. His Conductor reaches a wider audience. His Storyteller allows him to craft the message for the greatest impact. His Inner Advisor allows him to question what is happening around him. We discuss him here through the lens of a Social Practitioner (Understanding and Communication). However, it is clear his Ethical Specialist is also engaged. This opens him up to also being a Prudent and Just Practitioner too. This reveals in other actions, such as his campaigns for equity for those living in a consumerist society, his significant donations towards Citizen Advice, and even the funding of a thinktank to look at the connection of mental health problems to debt.

Shadows of Social Practitioners:

Leadership Vice: Foolish

Blind Spots: Loud and Aloof

The Leadership Vice of Foolish results from the lack of both Understanding and Communication. Decisions are uninformed and relayed clumsily. Misinformation, misunderstanding, and miscommunication are common. The complete absence of these components of Social Practitioner leads to confusion and error. Even with good intentions, people can be led astray, and the implementation of ideas is poor.

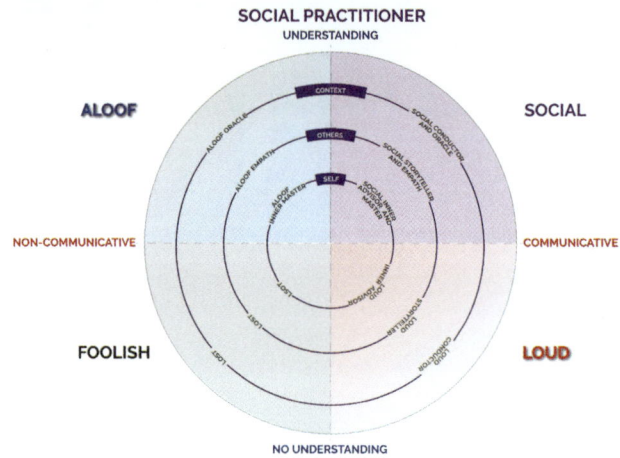

The Blind Spots result from the lack of either Understanding or Communication. The absence of Understanding (but with Communication) leads to the Blind Spot of Loud. Messages are fired out without checking sources or considering consequences. There is no coherent 'Communication strategy.' U-turns, corrections, and clarification become necessary. There is no alignment with the brand or other organisational guidelines.

The absence of Communication (but with Understanding) leads to the Blind Spot of Aloof. Well-crafted plans get left unimplemented. Stakeholders are unaware of the strategic direction of the organisation. Actions are taken in a bubble with little or no connection with those they affect. Teams become detached and complain of being 'left out'. People in power are perceived as less approachable. Even the best decisions can become misunderstood.

Let's look again at Martin Lewis. Imagine he used his journalistic nous without having Understanding. The 'loudness' of his messages would get heard. Everyone is interested in reducing their financial burdens but what if the messages were simply 'hot air'? His messages would have no substance. Unfortunately, in these days of fake news and bombastic rhetoric, those who shout the loudest get noticed. Algorithms used on social media regurgitate news that people are already looking at. Thus, the loudness of messages is mistaken as 'truth.' People do not always stop to test Understanding and can be misinformed and misled. In this scenario, Martin's behaviour would be Loud. High Communication/Low Understanding.

Alternatively, imagine he was unable to Communicate his message well. He sees the injustice, knows how to tackle it, but cannot find the platforms to spread his message. Perhaps he is overcautious, has no sense of timing, is overthinking things, and never vocalising them. His knowledge is not shared, and his behaviour is Aloof. High Understanding/Low Communication.

Finally, imagine he was devoid of both. He makes clumsy pronouncements about things he does not Understand and rushes in with ill-formed and ill-informed advice. Those who listen, perhaps the most vulnerable and desperate for guidance for their predicaments, lose more. Over time, the Foolishness reveals. He either falls from grace or reinvents himself as the 'witty fool.' Being Foolish can make problems worse through being clumsy, insensitive, and irresponsible. Theresa May, the then Prime Minister of the UK, was accused of failing to show "humanity" by Micheal Portillo during the Grenfell Tower fire of 2017. On her visit to the Grenfell site, she did not meet with survivors of the blaze. One year on, she herself described her actions as 'not good enough.' She failed to Understand the situation that she was presented with. Reflecting on the anniversary of the fire, she says, *"The residents of Grenfell Tower needed to know that those in power recognised and understood their despair."* She continues, *"...I will always regret that by not meeting them that day, it seemed as though I didn't care."* A poor Understanding of the real need for her visit led to her showing a lack of Empathy and sending the wrong message to those most in need of support at that time. Low Understanding leads to no Communication.

Being Foolish can lead to costly errors or sub-optimal impact of good intentions. One such example is that of a public health project in India. The Swachh Bharat Mission, launched in 2014, was to ensure open defecation in India became a thing of the past. Hundreds of thousands of latrines were installed throughout both rural and urban areas. However, behavioural norms were not considered. Villagers complained that they have had toilets installed, but no water. In Kharwada village in Rajasthan's Sirohi district, toilet blocks were used by residents as storage sheds and workshops instead. In urban slums in Navrangpura in Ahmedabad, users had to pay to use the facilities, many continued to relieve themselves in the open due to not wanting or affording to pay. Rinku Kumari, who worked on the project, commented, *"The tough part sometimes starts after the toilet is built. It is getting people to use them. People have to be convinced first that they need to use the toilet. We try to tell them about the spread of disease due to open defecation and make them aware of the advantages of better sanitation."* A need for both sensitive Understanding and appropriate Communication.

Theatre directing is a context in which the importance of the Social Practitioner also comes to the fore. Actors need to be both brave and vulnerable in the moment to moment unfolding of a play on stage. A theatre director must create the best environment for them to do so. They need to Understand their performers, their fears, ambitions, strengths, and weaknesses. They need to Understand the audience, their expectations, likes, and dislikes.

They need to Understand the theatre house, its opportunities, and limitations. They also need to Communicate with their actors, guiding and inspiring them. The job of rehearsal is to do this constantly. The play itself needs to Communicate the desired emotion and nuance to the audience for appropriate impact. The director also Conducts messages through lighting, set, costume, and sound design. Done well, they become expert Social Practitioners.

Whilst possessing the Leadership Vice of Foolish, you are unable to 'level up' to any of the other Virtue Practitioners except Spiritual (which requires Ethics and Purpose only). As such, it is possible to be a Spiritual Practitioner and be Foolish.

To avoid these leadership shadows and become a Social Practitioner, the natural flow of information between the Specialists of Understanding and Communication needs to be nurtured. One possesses static energy whilst the other is dynamic. One is a Grounding Specialist, and the other is a Growth Specialist. However, for these two Specialists, dialogue can be free flowing as they assist one another's development.

The Just Practitioner

Just Practitioners are Specialists in Ethics and Communication. This combination allows them to champion what is right. They hold strong, principled positions and are not afraid to articulate them. Each Specialist enhances the other to reveal the Leadership Virtue of Just.

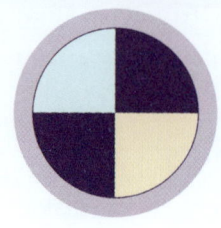

Just Practitioner knows what is right and defends it, 'walking the talk' and 'talking the walk'. A champion of worthy causes, articulating values well, and convincing others to support them. Communication is authentic and spoken from the heart. What is right is right, and advocated without fear. Just Practitioner is fair, equitable, persuasive, and believable. This allows confidence and character to be bold in the pursuit of righteousness. **The Just Practitioner holds fast to Ethics and knows how to persuasively Communicate them.** Just Practitioner is eloquent and delivers messages with clarity and coherence. Reactions and responses are listened to in order to gather further evidence to support or correct arguments. Feedback is welcomed and direction is corrected if needed. **The Just Practitioner Communicates expertly to further their Ethical position and awareness.** A perpetual seeker of truth, their information is filtered through a prism of deeply held values, and their responses are measured against a moral compass.

Just Inner Referee and Inner Advisor

In the Domain of Self, Inner Referee gives steer to Inner Advisor; and Inner Advisor gives Inner Referee the tools and time for reflection. In combination, the Just Practitioner of the Domain of Self is a reflective and righteous Practitioner.

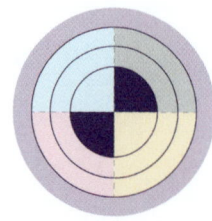

Statements and behaviour are aligned with values. Intention and action are self-checked, and changed if found lacking in complete integrity. Conscious and unconscious bias is managed. Beliefs are reflected upon, truths philosophised, and the meaning of life contemplated.

Just Mentor and Storyteller

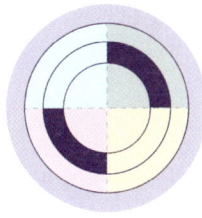

In the Domain of Others, Mentor gives Storyteller the opportunity to positively influence others; and Storyteller gives Mentor the language to do so. In combination, the Just Practitioner of the Domain of Others is an eloquent guide. Messages are crafted to penetrate the conscience of the receiver, using beautiful words, gestures, and tones. Verses and metaphors are powerfully used to illustrate principle-centred stories. Others are illuminated through flexibility and fluency in language, and role-modelling. A righteous guru for those seeking to elevate their morality, others are directed towards goodness and what is right. Equality and truth are advocated, articulated, and represented.

Just Custodian and Conductor

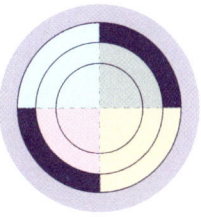

In the Domain of Context, Custodian gives Conductor the opportunity to spread goodness in the world; and Conductor gives Custodian the ability to cast its message wider. In combination, the Just Practitioner of the Domain of Context both creates and inspires a positive legacy. Competency with the use of Communication platforms allow high integrity messages to proliferate. Principled organisations are built, and clarity ensured with regards to the 'code of conduct' in them. Minorities, underprivileged, or the oppressed are given a voice. Universal human rights, fairness, and righteousness are championed, validated, amplified, and elevated. Communities are mobilised to stand up for universal truths. "Injustice anywhere is a threat to justice everywhere" (Martin Luther King Jr.) is the mantra. Values must prevail for everyone, not just a few. The law is guarded when it is Just, and fiercely opposed when it is not.

The Just Practitioner in action

The seventieth anniversary of the UN Universal Declaration of Human Rights was in 2019. The Declaration was the first step in formulating the International Bill of Human Rights, which came into force in 1976. The document communicates, at a global level, the rights of individuals, and stands as a constitution for Just Practitioners. The political prisoner/activist/artist Ai WeiWei designed a flag to commemorate the anniversary, which was flown by organisations across the world. Ai WeiWei's inspiration for the design of the flag came from his visit to a Rohingya refugee camp, where he noticed people without shoes. The flag displays a 'bare footprint.' The image serves as a reminder that universal human rights must be secured for everyone. At the launch of the 'Fly the Flag' project, Ai WeiWei reminded people that we must both know about human rights (Ethics) and Communicate them (Just Practitioner). He emphasises that when we notice rights being violated in any part of the world, our own rights are also being violated. The 'Fly the Flag' project encouraged everybody to join in the conversation about Universal Human Rights. People were invited to record a speech, poem, or story and post it on social media. Campaigners of this type fit the Just Practitioner definition. High Ethics/High Communication. Martin Luther King Jr., Malcolm X, and Mahatma Gandhi all campaigned for the rights of minorities or the oppressed, highlighted the injustice, and then expertly used the Communication tools of their time.

The 14th Dalai Lama, Tenzin Gyatso, is a Just Practitioner, campaigning for the Tibetan people in exile. Despite significant obstacles, he remains steadfast in his articulation of what is right. The Dalia Lama is the spiritual leader of the Tibetan people. Buddhists believe in the principle of reincarnation, and that the Dalai Lama can choose the body into which he is reincarnated. This is historically overseen by monks. However, the Chinese government is now able to supervise this reincarnation. Faced with a difficult decision with regards to his successor in the face of the Chinese control of Tibet, the spiritual leader has hinted that he might be the last person to hold the title of Dalai Lama. In a statement released in 2011, he said it was inappropriate for the Chinese government to supervise his reincarnation. *"They say they are waiting for my death and will recognise a 15th*

Dalai Lama of their choice. It is clear from their recent rules and regulations and subsequent declarations that they have a detailed strategy to deceive Tibetans." He said he would consult with his fellow monks when he was *"about 90"* on whether the institution of the Dalai Lama should continue. Just Practitioners are bold to make the right decision. They may not be understood nor popular, but they are values-based and principled.

Shadows of Just Practitioners:

Leadership Vice: Dangerous

Blind Spots: Reclusive and Deceiving

The Leadership Vice of Dangerous results from the lack of both Ethics and Communication. Speech can be clumsy, crass, vulgar, and obnoxious. Attempts to misguide and misdirect are constantly made. A complete absence of these components of Just can lead to wrongful convictions and oppression. Systems are abused and opportunities are withheld. Wicked and even criminal intent can flourish.

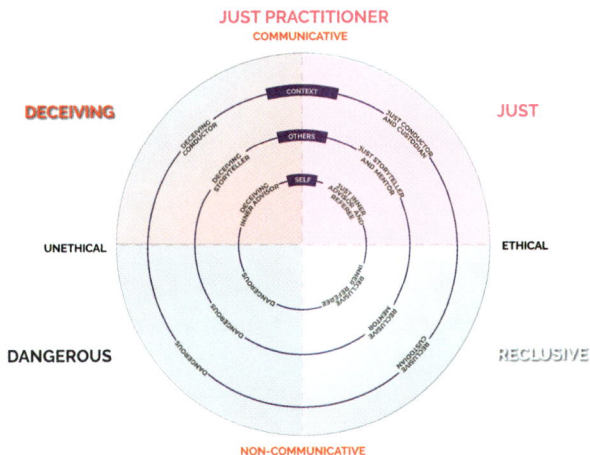

The Blind Spots result from the lack of either Ethics or Communication. The absence of Ethics (but with Communication) leads to the Blind Spot of Deceiving. Messages are dishonest, fake, or designed to trick the receiver. Self-justification for wrongdoing is common. Communication channels are abused for self-interest, and for spreading conflict. Spin doctoring becomes the norm. A silver tongue is used to mislead and misguide with irresponsible enticements and false promises.

The absence of Communication (but with Ethics) leads to the Blind Spot of Reclusive. Miscarriages of justice remain unchallenged. Values or contributions remain unshared. Followers cannot access the guidance they seek. Edmund Burke famously said, *"All that is required for evil to triumph is for good men to do nothing."* The Recluse will do and say nothing. For a Recluse, values and principles become a private matter. You may use a refillable water bottle or recycle; ride your bicycle to work to lower your carbon footprint; do unto others as you would have done on to yourself; give charity to the homeless; dream of peace and have a conscience - but never articulate or share these things. This is the behaviour of a Recluse. High Ethics/Low Communication. If these values are essential, why would you not wear them on your sleeve, and wish others to sign up for them too? If there are no campaigners to tackle climate change, how will the message be heard? If there is no one speaking out against oppression, then how will the situation change? Archbishop Desmond Tutu once said, *"If you are neutral in situations of injustice, you have chosen the side of the oppressor. If an elephant has its foot on the tail of a mouse and you say that you are neutral, the mouse will not appreciate your neutrality."*

Aesop's fable of the 'wolf in sheep's clothing' is a story that captures Deceiving well. In Matthew's gospel, the bible also warns, *"Beware of false prophets, which come to you in sheep's clothing, but inwardly they are ravening (hungry) wolves."* Modern day fairy tales like Little Red Riding Hood also warn of false disguises and Deceiving words. In all the above, low Ethics is disguised through high (false) Communication. Fake news, rumour, and slander are becoming more and more commonplace. The internet allows highspeed Communication without any concern for Ethics. Regulating it is a challenge, and he who shouts loudest, irrespective of integrity, gets heard.

Donald Trump's presidency, from January 2017 – January 2021, gives us many examples to show both Dangerous and Deceiving in practice. James Robison, the televangelist, describes him: *"It's as though Trump has the charisma, the pied-piper effect, and could lead the whole nation off the cliff, and they would think they were on the way to Disney World."* This is him in his

Deceiving state. His ability to use social media, position, and business standing served him well on occasion. However, clumsy language and 'shooting from the hip' means the same platforms expose him too. His Dangerous comments about the use of the drug Hydroxychloroquine during the 2020 Covid-19 pandemic, where his tweets prompted a 'factcheck' notice by Twitter (X), or his statement to Fox News in 2011 about Obama, *"He doesn't have a birth certificate. He may have one, but there's something on that, maybe religion, maybe it says he is a Muslim"* as a malicious attempt to stoke Islamophobic sentiment - both prompting outrage and a backlash due to bad intention and inept articulation. His subsequent presidency was full of similar displays, for example, his claims that President Volodymyr Zelensky of Ukraine is a 'dictator without elections' or that he started the war with Russia.

Whilst possessing the Leadership Vice of Dangerous, you are unable to 'level up' to any of the other Virtue Practitioners except Wise (which requires Understanding and Purpose only). As such, it is possible to be a Wise Practitioner and be Dangerous.

To avoid these leadership shadows and become a Just Practitioner, there needs to be a constant connection between the Specialists in Ethics and Communication. One possesses static energy whilst the other is dynamic. One is a Grounding Specialist, and the other is a Growth Specialist. Working together, they embolden each other.

The Spiritual Practitioner

Spiritual Practitioners are Specialists in Purpose and Ethics. This combination ensures the chosen path is ambitious yet meaningful. That the future intended and worked towards, is wholesome and positive. Each Specialist enhances the other to reveal the Leadership Virtue of Spiritual.

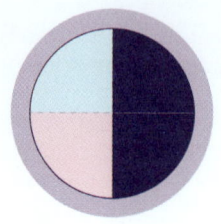

The competency in change-making is used to right wrongs. Innovation is applied to resolve challenges of injustice, inequity, and prejudice. **The Spiritual Practitioner has an Ethical Purpose.** Morality and principles inform problem-solving, and belief becomes a motivator for action. **The Spiritual Practitioner is Purposefully Ethical.** Direction is 'checked out' for correctness using value-based standards. The answers provided are beneficial and proper. What is helpful for people and society is favoured. The combination of vision and values provides a path that transcends the conventional.

Spiritual Inner Visionary and Inner Referee

In the Domain of Self, Inner Visionary gives the Inner Referee challenges of new dilemmas to assess; and Inner Referee gives Inner Visionary its integrity. In combination, the Spiritual Practitioner of the Domain of Self is both determined and tenacious. There is a moral map, a moral destination, and a moral compass. Applying principles to make a positive change is motivating and made with firm intentions. The heart is at peace, optimistic, and confident. Goals are achieved whilst also being caring, forgiving, decent, and helpful.

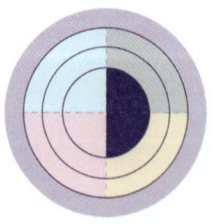

Spiritual Navigator and Mentor

In the Domain of Others, Navigator gives the Mentor information useful for assisting others; and Mentor gives Navigator a standard for measuring the correctness of another's direction. In combination, the Spiritual Practitioner of the Domain of Others is an upright guide.

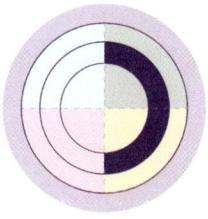

Interventions and advice build character and move people towards their desired goals. Road maps are sought to steer others through the moral maze of life. People are inspired to leave beneficial legacies and supported through the journey. Plans are exciting whilst also remaining congruent with values. Devotion is given and received. Like iron filings to a magnet, attraction is towards both substance and direction, not just words.

Spiritual Architect and Custodian

In the Domain of Context, Architect gives Custodian the opportunity to shape a constructive future; and Custodian gives Architect a measure of the moral consequences of change. In combination, the Spiritual Practitioner of the Domain of Context provides hope and aspiration. Productive and principle centred futures are constructed. Faith in a mission, a community of believers, and a route to achieving goals is given. Change is facilitated whilst still caring for the environment, culture, inclusion, and minorities. Nature, nurture, and humanity are considered. The focus is not just on the worldly growth of a company or society, but on the character of the people too.

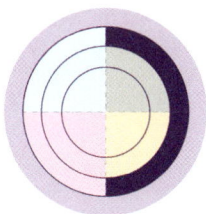

The Spiritual Practitioner in action

Spiritual Practitioners are all around us. Good people direct others towards good things. They are known to those in their 'circle of influence' but do not boast beyond those boundaries. As such, we may not always hear about them. The ones we hear about are usually those that are also Communication Specialists. This not only gives a voice to the Spiritual Practitioner but also releases the Leadership Virtues of Justice and Courage too. This voice can often be found due to adversity (often the same adversity giving them Purpose). The need to speak out to prevent harm, achieve the desired vision, or safeguard a fundamental right.

One example of adversity creating a Spiritual Practitioner is Malala Yousafzai. As a young child of a school teacher, she valued education. When the Taliban in the Swat Valley prevented her from going to school, she chose to speak out (a Spiritual, Courageous, and Just Practitioner). She was shot in the head because of this. She survived, following months of surgery and rehabilitation, and now continues her Ethical Purpose to ensure every girl can go to school. In recognition of her work, she became the youngest ever recipient of the Nobel Peace Prize in 2014. Her Malala Foundation now supports the education of thousands of girls. She is a Mentor, Navigator, and role model for them. Her work promotes human rights for women globally. Malala's drive comes from knowing what is right and having the determination to make a change to see it manifest in the world. Gandhi famously said, *"Be the change you want to see in the world."* Malala's story shows us how.

Shadows of Spiritual Practitioners:

Leadership Vice: Adrift

Blind Spots: Pedantic and Devious

The Leadership Vice of Adrift results from the lack of both Purpose and Ethics. Actions are without integrity and resolve. They are meaningless and insincere. A complete absence of these components of the Spiritual leads to pointless and empty gestures. Value is lost. Advice is disingenuous and points in the wrong direction.

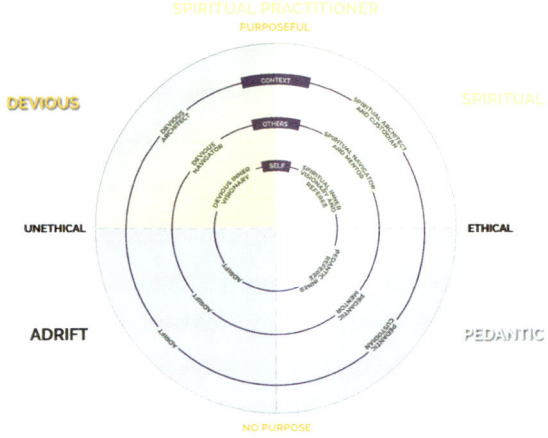

The Blind Spots result from the lack of either Purpose or Ethics. The absence of Purpose (but with Ethics) leads to the Blind Spot of Pedantic. Actions are well intended, but do not actually contribute towards acquiring the desired goal. Progress is frustrated due to rigidity and nitpicking. The relevance of belief is lost due to a lack of connection to meaning.

The absence of Ethics (but with Purpose) leads to the Blind Spot of Devious. Misdirection is used for personal gain. Conflicts of interest are common. Power and position are abused. Nepotism and prejudice persist. Bullying, coercion, and oppression are allowed.

In 2016, the UK voted to leave the European Union. The then Prime Minister, David Cameron, resigned. His successor, Theresa May, was tasked to see through the public vote. Without any clear picture of a post EU Britain, she adopted a mantra of *"Brexit means Brexit"*, and triggered Article 50 (setting a timeline for the exit). Her actions were motivated by a commitment to see the 'democratic will of the people' through. Whether one voted to remain or leave, the lack of vision led to confusion, uncertainty, and resignations. She lay down red lines only to concede on them in negotiations.

Her own party rebelled against her, and she went on to lose the confidence of parliament, being defeated at every 'meaningful vote.' The UK was forced to keep going back to Brussels to extend the Brexit timelines.

In June 2019, she stood down as Prime Minister. Her actions displayed the Pedantic shadow. Holding onto the value of "Brexit means Brexit" without knowing what to do with it, how to advance it or what the destination looks like. This Pedantic shadow shows the peril of values without vision, being well intentioned but without a direction to apply it. High Ethics/Low Purpose.

Devious is the shadow at work during horrific acts such as genocide. Adolf Eichmann was described as the 'Architect of the Holocaust.' He devised and coordinated the details that saw millions of Jewish people sent to their deaths. The efficiency with which he systematised the transportation and extermination of people made him the most feared man in the Nazi regime. During his trial, he reportedly said that he was simply obeying orders in a totalitarian regime. He showed neither remorse nor responsibility for his actions. Without values, a vision will be corrupt and evil. High Purpose/Low Ethics.

Those who are Adrift are often used by those who are Devious. They become their foot soldiers. Directionless and with low integrity, they are easily tempted to associate with the power of a dictator. In 1963, Stanley Milgram, a psychologist, conducted an experiment. He described it as follows, *"I set up a simple experiment at Yale University to test how much pain an ordinary citizen would inflict on another person simply because he was ordered to, by an experimental scientist. Stark authority was pitted against the subjects' strongest moral imperatives against hurting others, and, with the subjects' ears ringing with the screams of the victims, authority won more often than not."*

The experiment shows what happens when the agency to make one's own moral decisions is compromised. The subjects had to follow another's direction. They were also assured they were doing the right thing. "It is absolutely essential that you continue," being the instruction given by authorities. As such, they disabled personal Purpose and Ethics, leaving them Adrift to be used by those with the power. No Ethics/No Purpose. A Spiritual Practitioner would be able to Navigate through such challenges and be a Custodian of their own and others' values.

Whilst possessing the Leadership Vice of Adrift, you are unable to 'level up' to any of the other Virtue Practitioners except Social (which requires Understanding and Communication only). As such, it is possible to be a Social Practitioner and be Adrift.

To avoid these leadership shadows and become a Spiritual Practitioner there needs to be a symbiotic relationship between the Specialists of Purpose and Ethics. One possesses static energy whilst the other is dynamic. One is a Grounding Specialist, and the other is a Growth Specialist. The Ethical Specialist anchors the Purpose Specialist whilst the latter drives the former into action.

The Courageous Practitioner

Courageous Practitioners are Specialists in Purpose and Communication. This combination allows them to be bold in action. They see clearly where they want to be and can influence others to help them get there. Each Specialist enhances the other to reveal the Leadership Virtue of Courage.

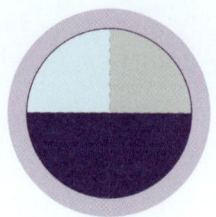

A vision of the future is crafted and articulated, moving heart and body into action. Coalitions are built and teams are inspired. **The Courageous Practitioner is audacious, confident, motivational, and persuasive.** Causes are advanced with determination, embracing daring and risk, if needed. A 'silver tongue' is enhanced with attractive stories of 'pots of gold' at the end of the rainbow. **The Courageous Practitioner has a Purpose and is convincing whilst Communicating it.** Language is articulate, responsive, and flexible. Others are aroused and stirred into action. The Courageous Practitioner Communicates well to advance their Purpose. Change is constantly moving from milestone to milestone, seeking new ideas and opportunities.

Courageous Inner Visionary and Inner Advisor

In the Domain of Self, Inner Visionary gives Inner Advisor direction; and Inner Advisor motivates Inner Visionary. The Courageous Practitioner of the Domain of Self is both reflective and sharp-witted. Focused and ambitious. Goals are known and progress towards them is measured. Most roads will do, if they are heading in the right direction, and passion may justify an end by any means.

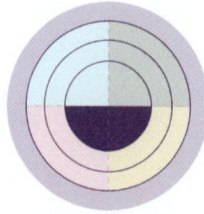

Courageous Navigator and Storyteller

In the Domain of Others, Navigator gives Storyteller the opportunity to inspire others; and Storyteller gives back the language with which to do it. In combination, the Courageous Practitioner of the Domain of Others is an articulate catalyst for change. Arguments are influential, exciting, inciting, and attractive. Rhetoric is used to stir and awaken the desire for change. Verse, expression, and style combined with adaptability provides the power to win people over.

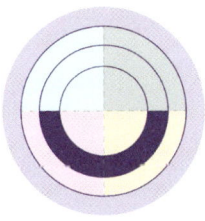

Courageous Architect and Conductor

In the Domain of Context, Architect gives Conductor the opportunity to inspire widely; and Conductor gives Architect the platforms to do so. In combination, the Courageous Practitioner of the Domain of Context is a powerful change-maker. Multiple Communication platforms are used to mobilise a vision community.

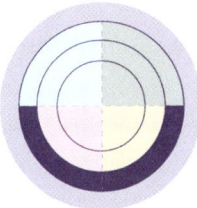

Organisations are agile, continually improving, and adapting to new circumstances. Drive, proactivity, creativity, and innovation are at the core of team working. Experimentation and technology are embraced. Motivational messages are widespread. People are aware of the direction of travel and are enthused about the journey. Brave steps are taken, and adaptive 'fix as you go' policies are adopted; however, vision is clear, and the ability to inspire is too. The Courageous Practitioner in the Domain of Context recognises that there is no better time to start than right now. 'Fortune favours the bold' is the mantra.

The Courageous Practitioner in action

To be a Courageous Practitioner requires consistency in the small, as well as the big gestures. Let's consider the numerous opportunities life presents to become Courageous. Ordinary things, like asking someone out to dinner, or apologising to your spouse. Both require Purpose and Communication. Your Inner Advisor thinks about it, but unless your Inner Visionary validates it, you don't act. What if it was your friend who wanted the date or to resolve a conflict? Your Navigator would provide the motivation, but your Storyteller would need to move them from inaction to action.

What if the relationship or conflict resolution was required at an organisational or societal level? Your Architect would lay out the aspired future, but your Conductor would need to mobilise the vision community to make it a reality. All these scenarios require action. Communication is a form of action, and action is a form of Communication. The value created by pairing these Specialists enables people to act despite the risk. As the cliché says: 'feel the fear and do it anyway.' The Courageous Practitioner is bold in reaching out to others to garner support for their desired goals.

A head teacher at a special school recently used her weekly 'town hall' session to Communicate an unpopular, or so she thought, message to staff. The session took place after a particularly hard-hitting TV documentary about the maltreatment of adults with high support needs in the care system. The school has many such pupils who have repeated violent outbursts towards staff. Many felt demoralised by the challenges these pupils brought and were fearful for their own personal safety. They wanted these pupils excluded, as is the practice in other schools. Yet, the head teacher took the opportunity to recommend they watch the documentary to understand why the policy in this school was to keep the most challenging pupils within the school environment. Giving them all the same opportunities to engage in activities, such as school trips or Duke of Edinburgh awards, as other pupils. The head teacher Communicated her belief that the school environment is the most significant way to influence the life outcomes of these pupils. To exclude them, would be to assign them to a permanent lifetime of low-quality care, and potential largescale abuse. There is, in her words, nowhere to go if you are excluded from a special school. In her speech, she recognised that the decision to keep the pupils in school was difficult, challenging, and unconventional. *"And we do it anyway because it fits our vision and purpose as an educational establishment that provides equality of opportunity to all our pupils".* From then on, the staff connected to their Purpose in a new way. Motivation and engagement were never higher. There was a buzz in the air and staff and pupils alike felt uplifted. There is no doubt that there is a level of Understanding and Ethics in this story too. However, we use it to highlight how she used Purpose and Communication courageously.

Shadows of Courageous Practitioners:

Leadership Vice: Mute

Blind Spots: Noisy and Frustrated

The Leadership Vice of Mute results from the lack of both Purpose and Communication. Inaction results, and messages are dull and boring. Work becomes tedious and monotonous. Tasks are repetitive with little or no imagination or excitement. A complete absence of these components of Courageous can lead to stagnation and isolation. Progress is stunted, and people feel insignificant and demoralised.

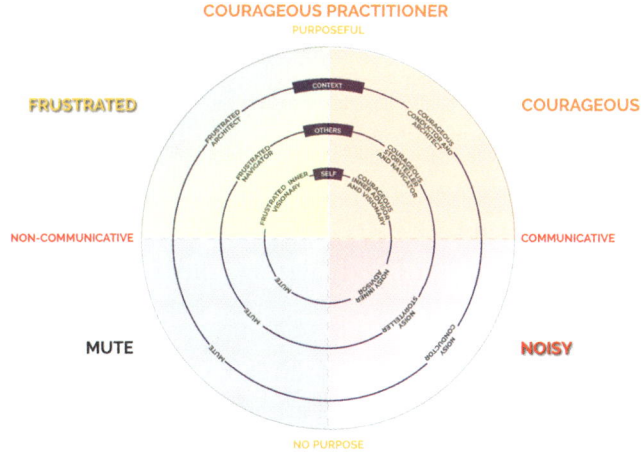

The Blind Spots result from the lack of either Purpose or Communication. The absence of Purpose (but with Communication) leads to the Blind Spot of Noisy. Instructions are incoherent and lack clear direction. Mixed messages and U-turns are common. Confusion arises as people 'miss the point.' Aimless sound bites are produced. People feel as lost, after having received instructions, as they did beforehand.

The absence of Communication (but with Purpose) leads to the Blind Spot of being Frustrated. Opportunities remain unexplored, and inventions are wasted. Ideas are not shared, and communities do not assemble to make them a reality. Action is not taken, and visions remain as frustrated dreams.

Noisy is well illustrated in conjecture and gossip. The tabloid press is great at it. Stories with no meaningful Purpose fill pages, and often, such Noisy Communications play to primitive emotions. They can be very damaging. One such example is that of the Blue Whale Challenge. It followed the unfortunate suicide of Rina Palenkova in south-eastern Russia, in November 2015. Speculation and 'noise' around her death, and that of other teenagers, led to a plethora of online theories to emerge. A frenzy followed, which culminated in an article by journalist Galina Mursalieva which sent the story into overdrive. The Blue Whale Suicide Challenge was born. The world was shocked. The challenge was reported to encourage young people to harm themselves, with the final challenge being to take their own life. The police, public health authorities, and support services in many countries issued warnings - with parents and teachers being on full alert. Three years later, it was revealed that the whole thing was a hoax and there was no such thing as a Blue Whale Challenge. Noisy Communication had spread Purposeless gossip. There is some truth in the adage, 'empty vessels make the most noise.' High Communication/Low Purpose.

In 2017, the journalist Emma Freud ran a Twitter experiment. She asked people to share their biggest regrets. The result was over 300 replies sharing people's frustrations. The times they never acted when they knew they should have. Not communicating with loved ones towards the end of their lives. Not speaking out against abuse. Not taking advantage of the opportunities education provided. Fearing to say what needed to be said to take advantage of openings. Freud relates, *"A few tweets from people regretting that they had declared their love and ended up having their heartbroken, but many, many more regretting not being braver, and not risking vulnerability, the regret of having been afraid"*. Dreams are left unfulfilled. Low Communication/High Purpose.

The inaction accompanying being Mute can lead to dangerous consequences. Decisions that are critical for the wellbeing of people, organisations, and society are put off. Let's take the issue of gun control in the US. The untimely death of innocent victims, especially in schools, necessitates action, but there is no agreement on what the change needed should be. A Purpose cannot be agreed upon. Democrats call for tighter gun control, whilst Republicans quote the second amendment. This does, at first, sound like there is a debate and thus, Communication is happening, however, no one is actually listening. In fact, when a shooting happens and emotions are running high, the debate is often Muted. Republicans call the Democrats insensitive for talking about gun control 'at a time like this' when all thoughts should be with the families of the victims and not on politics. Political procrastination results. Low Purpose/Low Communication.

To avoid these leadership shadows and become a Courageous Practitioner, the Specialists in Purpose and Communication must collaborate. They are both dynamic energies which makes them transformational. They are both Growth Specialists. Working together, they enable one another.

Master Practitioners

The Twelve Characters in Good Leadership work in a relationship with each other. These relationships of 'joining up' allow them to further 'level up' and release Leadership Virtues that enhance them. Without these relationships, they manifest their shadows. Virtue Practitioners must now combine to level up even further to Master Practitioners. It is only through this ongoing collaboration that they rise to the level of a Good Leader.

> *"Coming together is a beginning; keeping together is progress; working together is success."*
> **Henry Ford**

- A Prudent Practitioner that develops Communication will unlock a Social Practitioner and a Just Practitioner.
- A Prudent Practitioner that develops Purpose will unlock a Wise and Spiritual Practitioner.
- A Courageous Practitioner that develops Ethics will unlock a Just and Spiritual Practitioner.
- A Courageous Practitioner that develops Understanding will unlock a Wise and Social Practitioner.

Each Master Practitioner possesses the qualities associated with the Leadership Virtue Practitioners that make it up. Yet, each still carries a shadow due to the last missing Specialist.

Good Leadership is about the future. It is about change. Prudence, Social and Just without Purpose will still stunt progress towards a desired future, and the long-term change needed.

Good Leadership is about influence. Prudence, Wise and Spiritual without Communication lacks the tools for moving people in a desired direction.

Good Leadership is about adding value and capacity. Courage, Just and Spiritual without Understanding lacks the insights required to ensure long-term sustainability in the value and capacity created.

Good Leadership is about positive impact and legacies. Courage, Wise and Understanding without Ethics nurtures an environment for potential abuse, destructive impact, and wicked legacies.

Good Leadership is thus the Learning, Loving, Leading, and Living of all Twelve Characters. This results in the emergence of all four Specialists and all six Leadership Virtue Practitioners. This allows the emergence of Good Leadership.

CHAPTER 4
SHOWING UP

> "Example is not the main thing in influencing others. It is the only thing."
> **Albert Schweitzer**

SHOWING UP

Good Leadership can be observed all around us. To highlight Good Leadership in practice, let's look at three Good Leaders. We view these showcases through the lens of Leadership Virtue Practitioners that bring balance to each other.

Wisdom (a combination of Understanding and Purpose) is balanced by Justice (a combination of Ethics and Communication). This balance is achieved because these two Leadership Virtue Practitioners involve all four Specialists. As such, their combination unlocks all the other Leadership Virtue Practitioners, and thus, Good Leadership. We look at Jacinda Ardern through these two Virtue Practitioners, and show how mastering these two Virtues unlocks the remaining four.

Social (a combination of Understanding and Communication) is balanced by Spiritual (a combination of Ethics and Purpose). We look at Yusuf Cat Stevens through these two Virtue Practitioners, and show how mastering these two Virtues unlocks the remaining four.

Prudence (a combination of Understanding and Ethics) is balanced by Courage (a combination of Purpose and Communication). We look at Poppy Jaman through these two Virtue Practitioners, and show how mastering these two Virtues unlocks the remaining four.

In all three cases, the combination unlocks Good Leadership. As such, the possession of the balancing Leadership Virtues allows the practice of all the others too.

Jacinda Ardern

As the 40th Prime Minister of New Zealand, Jacinda Ardern became the world's youngest female head of government at the age of 37. Let's look at her Wisdom and Justice, and then how the combination unlocks the Leadership Virtues of Social, Spiritual, Prudence, and Courage too.

Wise Virtue Practitioner: In March 2019, 51 people were fatally shot and 49 injured in two mosques in Christchurch. Jacinda showed Wisdom in her handling of the crisis. She chose to wear a hijab in solidarity with the grieving Muslim community. *"My job is to make people feel safe."* It was, she said, *"an obvious decision."* She shows depth in her Understanding of the situation as an Oracle. She ensures comfort and rapport through her Empath. Her Inner Master is mature enough to be confident and comfortable with wearing the head covering. Her Purpose is to restore a vision of a peaceful and safe New Zealand. One shared by all New Zealanders, but in doubt for this particular community. She took Wise action to bring that vision to reality swiftly. *"What has happened in Christchurch is an extraordinary act of unprecedented violence. It has no place in New Zealand. Many of those affected will be members of our migrant communities. New Zealand is their home they are us."* she articulates. Her Inner Visionary is clear on what she wishes to achieve; she Navigates others to achieve the same common Purpose, and she reignites, as Architect, the greater goal of unity and security. Many people found her response to the Christchurch shootings inspirational. Others have criticised it. Either way, it achieved a desired Purpose with an Understanding of Self, Others, and Context. She acted with the Leadership Virtue of Wisdom.

Just Virtue Practitioner: In 2018, Jacinda brings her infant to the UN General Assembly. *"If I can do one thing, and that is change the way we think about these things, then I will be pleased we have achieved something,"* she said. The unprecedented action is a result of her confident Inner Referee, guiding her on what she believes to be important and right. She uses the platform to thus Communicate this, enabling her Mentor and Custodian to reach working women globally.

She comments, *"It is a woman's decision about when they choose to have children, and it should not predetermine whether or not they are given a job or have job opportunities."* She has also spoken publicly against human rights abuses against the Uyghur Muslim minority in China, and the Rohingya in Myanmar. Her actions were to Communicate her strongly held Ethics. She acted with the Leadership Virtue of Just.

From the above balancing Virtues, we can see she has developed the Specialists of Understanding, Ethics, Purpose and Communication. These unlock the other Leadership Virtues:

Social Virtue Practitioner: Her depth of Understanding combined with competency in Communication have allowed her to be effective, approachable, and empathetic in her use of social media. She comments, *"One of the criticisms I've faced over the years is that I'm not aggressive enough, or assertive enough, or maybe somehow, because I'm empathetic, it means I'm weak. I totally rebel against that. I refuse to believe that you cannot be both compassionate and strong."* This approach served her very well during the 2020 global Covid19 pandemic. A former prime minister of New Zealand, Helen Clark, comments on Jacinda's natural and Empathetic Communication, as giving people the feeling that she is *"standing with them."* She goes on to say, *"They may even think: 'Well, I don't quite understand why the government did that, but I know she's got our back.' There's a high level of trust and confidence in her because of that empathy."*

Spiritual Virtue Practitioner: Her strongly held Ethics and sense of Purpose guide her policies. She advocates that New Zealand must be on the *"right side of history"* and lead in areas such as climate change.

Her government passed legislation committing New Zealand to zero carbon emissions by 2050. She comments, *"Ultimately, I do want us to be a transformative government. I want, when we've left, for people to say we're not just clean-green anymore: we're carbon neutral."* Her government also steered New Zealand towards caring for those most vulnerable through policies around child poverty and social inequality. On taking office, she says, *"We aspire to be a government for all New Zealanders and one that will seize the opportunity to build a fairer, better New Zealand."*

Prudent Virtue Practitioner: Her Understanding of people and situations combined with strongly held Ethical positions helped ease strained relations with their neighbour Australia. In 2017, the Prime Minister of Australia commented, *"we trust each other. The fact we are from different political traditions is irrelevant."* A similar combination of information, intelligence, and empathy mixed with unflinching honesty helped her achieve some of the world's best results during the 2020 Covid19 pandemic. *"I am a thinker, and I do muse over things a lot, and am constantly assessing whether I am doing enough, or what I should be doing more of to make sure I am not letting anyone down."* she comments.

Courageous Virtue Practitioner: Her commitment to a Purpose and her ability to compose, and be composed with, effective Communication served her well when she was on camera during a 5.8 magnitude earthquake. *"We're just having a bit of an earthquake here we're fine, I'm not under any hanging lights."* she says as she continues with the TV interview on 25th May 2020 from Wellington. In what must have felt like Deja vu, a year later, on 22nd October 2021, at a coronavirus briefing, she grabbed her podium as a 5.9 magnitude earthquake shook Wellington. She smiled and told the reporter: *"Sorry, a slight distraction, would you mind repeating the question?"* Her confident and calming Communication anchored with her commitment to the Purpose for which she was there, driving her response.

SHOWING UP

Yusuf Cat Stevens

One of the most influential singer song writers of all time. Yusuf Cat Stevens has vast musical achievements, but he has also had a long-term spiritual quest. Let's look at his Social (worldly) and Spiritual Leadership Virtues, and then how the combination unlocks the other Leadership Virtues of Wisdom, Justice, Prudence, and Courage too.

Social Virtue Practitioner: With over five decades of experience in the music industry, his Understanding and Communication of, and in, the sector are significant. The period from 1970 to 1974 saw him ascend into the upper echelons of musical superstardom. His music resonates with audiences worldwide. Future generations continue to appreciate his songs, with their timeless quality shown when a cover of 'Father & Son' became a huge hit for the pop band Boyzone in the 1990s. The same song was later used in the Marvel film 'Guardians of the Galaxy 2'. He quotes on social media, *"There is a social need within our lives as human beings to have harmony."* Regarding his classic hit 'Peace Train,' he comments, *"Peace Train is a song I wrote, the message of which continues to breeze thunderously through the hearts of millions. There is a powerful need for people to feel that gust of hope rise-up again."* His Understanding and Communication Specialists working together to act with the Leadership Virtue of Social.

Spiritual Virtue Practitioner: In 1968, following a near-fatal bout of tuberculosis, he began his spiritual exploration. He was 20 years old. He transformed his life and music, writing songs such as 'Peace

Train,' 'Where Do the Children Play' and 'Morning has Broken'. From this point onwards, his life was as much about his charitable work and his messages of peace and unity, as it was his music. His conscience informed a new sense of Purpose. He established his own charities and was one of UNICEF's earliest celebrity Goodwill Ambassadors from the world of pop music. In 1975, he experienced yet another lifechanging event. Whilst swimming in the Pacific Ocean off Malibu, he began to be swept out to sea. Fearing imminent death, he called to God, pleading that should he be saved, he would dedicate his life to God's service. At that moment, a gentle wave delivered him to the shore safely, reinvigorating further his calling to serve a higher Purpose and maintain an Ethical lens on his life.

He has founded several further international humanitarian charities, set up educational institutions, and published books. Both publicly and privately, he invests tremendous resources into serving and supporting those in need. In 2003 Yusuf received the 'World Social Award' in Germany from an International World Awards Jury for 'dedicating his life to aiding the needy and the ill.' He is famously quoted as combining his Ethical thinking with direction and Purpose by saying, *"All things can be forgiven if we can progress."* He acts with the Leadership Virtue of Spiritual.

From the above balancing Virtues, we can see he has developed the Specialists of Understanding, Ethics, Purpose, and Communication. These unlock the other Leadership Virtues:

Wise Virtue Practitioner: His Understanding of the music industry has allowed him to leverage it to serve a greater Purpose. He was successfully able to transform himself and his assets to head in a preferred direction. He says, "To be what you want to be, you must give up being what you are."

Just Virtue Practitioner: The tragic events of 9/11 motivated Yusuf to, once again, take to the global stage. Strong Ethics and a Communication Specialism allowed him to speak out in the media against the atrocities, fanaticism, and war, and call for peace and unity. He began to perform some of his old repertoires again, notably 'Peace Train' on account of its message. He speaks openly about climate change, and environmental protection. In 2004 he was presented with the 'Man of Peace' award on behalf of a committee of Nobel peace laureates for having worked to *"alleviate the suffering of thousands of children and their parents, and dedicating himself to promoting peace, reconciling people, and the condemnation of terrorism."* He goes on to say, *"It's very difficult to ignore humanitarian disasters. The royalties from my albums continue to support my charity work."*

Prudent Virtue Practitioner: His Understanding of needs combined with his Ethical motivations have led to his launching the charitable initiative 'Peace Train' in 2020. With a vision of 'A World as One,' the organisation strives to 'Feed the Hungry and Spread Peace.' He is quoted as saying, *"Communal well-being is central to human life."* He works with local specialist partners to ensure the best possible interventions. Building capacity as he delivers bespoke programmes, keeping local communities involved in the design. He works domestically and internationally. Projects are sustainable, using solar power and locally sourced and recycled materials.

Courageous Virtue Practitioner: Despite his age (born 21st July 1948), he continues to use his Communication Specialism to advance his Purpose. Talking about his more recent concert tours, he says, *"I wouldn't be writing songs if I didn't have something to say."* He continues to perform live to tens of thousands of fans, including Glastonbury 2023.' Inspiring old and new generations with his message of peace.

Poppy Jaman

An internationally respected mental health advocate, national policy advisor, and social entrepreneur, Poppy is a global voice of authority on workplace mental health, and the CEO of the London 'City Mental Health Alliance' (CMHA). She was the co-founder of 'Mental Health First Aid' (MHFA) England and has sat as a non-executive director on the board of Public Health England. In the 2018 Queen's New Year's Honours List, Poppy was awarded an OBE in recognition of her services to people with mental health issues and, in 2019, was recognised by the FT readers as one of the year's game changing women. Let's look at her Prudence and Courage, and then how the combination unlocks the Leadership Virtues of Social, Spiritual, Wise, and Just too.

Prudent Virtue Practitioner: Her in-depth Understanding of mental health, combined with her Ethical struggle to ensure a workplace is a safe place for those experiencing mental health challenges, have led to her significant work with major employers in The City and beyond. In 2020 she tweeted, *"Today @CityMHA, along with the Bank of England, BSB, UK and the @TheFCA hosted a roundtable with 30 CEOs and directors from across the banking and financial services sector to exchange experiences of the impact of COVID-19 on mental health in the workplace. A critical issue."* Providing context and bringing her insights to the organisations, she leverages their power and inspires them to take responsibility for creating a positive legacy. She acted with the Leadership Virtue of Prudence.

Courageous Virtue Practitioner: She Communicates passionately about her Purpose. She shares her own experience of postnatal depression in her 20s to inspire others to do the same. She thus uses and encourages 'storytelling,' urging 'high-performance leaders' to come forward with their experiences to achieve the goal of helping more people. Her work is pioneering and innovative. In the summer of 2020, she joined other civil society leaders in a call to remove the word 'Empire' from the Honours system and replace it with 'Excellence.' *"I am a British Bangladeshi. This is my home. I've proudly dedicated my career to social good. I love my work, it is purpose-led. I represent British Excellence"* she tweets. The same drive to bring dramatic change to mental health that led to her receiving the Honour, is now motivating a drive to reform it. Her actions show a strong sense of Purpose, and the competence to Communicate it. She acted with the Leadership Virtue of Courageous.

From the above balancing Virtues, we can see she has developed the Specialists of Understanding, Ethics, Purpose, and Communication. These unlock the other Leadership Virtues:

Social Virtue Practitioner: Her depth of Understanding combined with competency in Communication have allowed her to deliver messages with credibility and persuasion. In 2017, after briefing the Prime Minister and cabinet on MHFA, the Secretary of State named her as one of England's mental health experts. She creates empathy and rapport through sharing her own personal stories. She presents not only the human case, but also the business case for firms in The City to take mental health seriously. *"We need understanding at the board level to create metrics and dashboards to measure success."* She calls for a culture of openness, *"Socially we are saying it is okay to not be okay. Outcomes of performance reviews will be different. Instead of looking at attendance and timekeeping, ask 'why?' and support employees. You will retain your talent".*

Spiritual Virtue Practitioner: Her Ethics and a sense of Purpose guide her work. *"Mental Health should not be stigmatised in the workplace. We know discrimination still exists…the whole mental health agenda has progressed so much in the last 40 years since the regulations were written. It (regulation) just* *does not reflect where society is at."* She has also supported the development of MHFA in Bangladesh. Poppy trained orphanage workers in mental health literacy in Goa. Her combined Ethics and Purpose inspired action.

Wise Virtue Practitioner: A strong sense of Purpose supported by an Understanding of the issues and interventions, led to the founding of MHFA England CIC. What started as a small government funded project, became a thriving Social Enterprise. In 2017, MHFA England was recognised by the Financial Times as one of the fastest growing SMEs in Europe. Wisdom is used to introduce longevity to work. Understanding the need for continued effort to achieve results, Poppy says, *"Until you win over hearts and minds change does not happen."*

Just Virtue Practitioner: In 2018, Poppy spearheaded 'Where's Your Head At'. A campaign for law changes to have mental health first aiders at work made compulsory. *"On an equalities level, it sends out the message that mental health should not be stigmatised in the workplace."* She goes on to say, *"We need to bring the agenda on a par with physical health."* She continues to be a voice for those experiencing poor mental health. She comments, "my fuel for life comes from the hardship, the health inequalities and injustice my community continue to experience." She continues to speak out, delivering lectures and performing interviews, campaigning for those experiencing mental health issues, and as a positive Asian female role model, inspiring future generations of the same.

CHAPTER 5
SUMMING UP

> "The end is just the beginning."
> **T.S. Eliot**

SUMMING UP

The Good Leadership Book takes you on a journey of Stepping Up into the Characters; Growing Up to Learn, Love, Lead and Live the Characters; Levelling Up to unleash Specialists; Joining Up as Virtue Practitioners to allow you to bring a complexity of response to the complexity of need; and finally Showing Up as a Good Leader.

Leadership is itself a continuous journey. Landscapes are constantly changing, and fresh challenges are presented at faster paces than at any time in history. We find ourselves in a world of pandemics, discriminatory 'isms,' disruptive technologies, growing divisions, and isolationism. Leaders need to steer through this voyage of unknown and uncertain territories, to reach a positive destination. As the seafaring stories from the ancient world tell us, embarking upon such a journey tests and expands human capabilities. It is both exhilarating and frightening: two sides of the same coin. Leadership is a 'call to adventure,' and The Good Leadership Model is a tool to help you directly, stay on course and complete your journey well.

The Model makes sure you are building trust and leading in all three Domains. Leading Self to provide resilience, steadfastness, motivation, and reflection, thus ensuring the captain is leading from a healthy place. Leading Others to give security, guidance, direction, and inspiration, thus ensuring those taking the journey with you are performing and developing as they travel along. Leading in Context to provide perspective, oversight, ambition, and connection, thus ensuring new terrains, opportunities, and threats are managed. Cutting across these Domains are the four Dimensions of Understanding, Ethics, Purpose, and Communication. The Grounding Dimensions of Understanding and Ethics create a strong, stabilising foundation for acting with agency in the world as it is, whilst the Growth Dimensions of Purpose and Communication bring clarity and shape to a desirable future.

The overlaps between these Domains and Dimensions reveal the Twelve Essential Characters of Leadership. Those in the Dimension of Understanding, helping to make sense of the **complexities** in the journey. This is where we find Inner Master giving emotional intelligence and stability, Empath helping to build rapport, and Oracle providing global insights.

Those in the Dimension of Ethics, help with anchors and principles to rely upon during the **uncertainties** in the journey. This is where we find Inner Referee providing a moral compass, Mentor acting as a positive guide, and Custodian ensuring respect.

Those in the Dimension of Purpose, provide focus and direction in a **volatile** journey. This is where we find Inner Visionary providing personal clarity, Navigator giving steer to others, and Architect bringing the community, resources, and assets together for a unified mission.

Those in the Dimension of Communication, help clarify the **ambiguities** in the journey. This is where we find Inner Advisor providing reflection, Storyteller a narrative and eloquence, and Conductor ensuring the conveyance of the leadership message.

> As adversity is known to 'build and reveal' character, leading in such times of uncertainty and rapid change requires you to 'build and reveal' these Twelve Characters.

Developing Depth in the Characters allows them to become instinctual and natural. To Live the Characters is to ensure they are habitual. This consistency in their application builds the 'complete trust' necessary in your Good Leadership. It is this 'complete trust' that will ensure the confidence in Self, the confidence of Others, and the confidence needed in an everchanging Context.

SUMMING UP

Complete /kuhm-pleet/ Adjective having all the necessary parts or elements; lacking nothing; whole; entire; full.		**Trust** /truhst/ Noun confidence; firm belief in the reliability of the integrity and ability of a person or thing.
Learn	Mind	Confidence in knowledge
Love	Heart	Confidence in passion and desire
Lead	Body	Confidence in doing
Live	Spirit	Confidence in the consistency of action

It is the coming together of these developed, 'depth-full', and thus trusted Characters that produce Specialists, and it is the coming together of these Specialists that reveal the Six Leadership Virtue Practitioners. These are Prudence, Courage, Justice, Wisdom, Spiritual and Social. As you journey towards Good Leadership, it is important for you to identify those areas of development that need attention. This not only helps you focus in terms of learning, but also helps you see your Vices and Blind Spots, the shadows that will sabotage and trip up your mission. Good Leaders are constant learners from the cradle to the grave. The more you learn, the more you often realise how much there is still to learn. The more you understand about a Character, the more you realise there is more to understand about each. The more you develop Depth in each Character, the more you understand that you can go deeper. The more you unlock Virtues, the more you realise that there is so much more to know. This is the perpetual leadership journey. This Model provides you with the comprehensive framework that you need to identify areas of development in your Good Leadership journey. In addition, it also provides you with a tool to identify what may be missing from your team, company, or community. As such, it can be used to inform recruitment to balance for skills and knowledge that are lacking in whole organisations. It is a complete guide with the ability to inform problem-solving, situational analysis, identify gaps, and direct personal and organisational growth. It has both depth and breadth. It can help you lock down and lift off; consolidate and expand; cultivate and evolve.